Four Corners

Jack C. Richards · David Bohlke

2A

Student's Book

CAMBRIDGE
UNIVERSITY PRESS

CAMBRIDGE
UNIVERSITY PRESS

32 Avenue of the Americas, New York NY 10013-2473, USA

Cambridge University Press is part of the University of Cambridge.

It furthers the University's mission by disseminating knowledge in the pursuit of education, learning and research at the highest international levels of excellence.

www.cambridge.org
Information on this title: www.cambridge.org/9780521126687

First published 2011
8th printing 2016

Printed in Dubai by Oriental Press

A catalog record for this publication is available from the British Library.

ISBN 978-0-521-12668-7 Full Contact 2A with Self-study CD-ROM
ISBN 978-0-521-12671-7 Full Contact 2B with Self-study CD-ROM
ISBN 978-0-521-12688-5 Teacher's Edition 2 with Assessment Audio CD / CD-ROM
ISBN 978-0-521-12681-6 Class Audio CDs 2
ISBN 978-0-521-12663-2 Classware 2
ISBN 978-0-521-12677-9 DVD 2

For a full list of components, visit www.cambridge.org/fourcorners

Cambridge University Press has no responsibility for the persistence or accuracy of URLs for external or third-party Internet Web sites referred to in this publication, and does not guarantee that any content on such Web sites is, or will remain, accurate or appropriate. Information regarding prices, travel timetables, and other factual information given in this work are correct at the time of first printing, but Cambridge University Press does not guarantee the accuracy of such information thereafter.

Art direction, book design, photo research, and layout services: Adventure House, NYC
Audio production: CityVox, NYC
Video production: Steadman Productions

Authors' acknowledgments

Many people contributed to the development of *Four Corners*. The authors and publisher would like to particularly thank the following **reviewers**:

Nele Noe, **Academy for Educational Development, Qatar Independent Secondary School for Girls**, Doha, Qatar; Yuan-hsun Chuang, **Soo Chow University**, Taipei, Taiwan; Celso Frade and Sonia Maria Baccari de Godoy, **Associaçao Alumni**, São Paulo, Brazil; Pablo Stucchi, **Antonio Raimondi School** and **Instituto San Ignacio de Loyola**, Lima, Peru; Kari Miller, **Binational Center**, Quito, Ecuador; Alex K. Oliveira, **Boston University**, Boston, MA, USA; Elisabeth Blom, **Casa Thomas Jefferson**, Brasilia, Brazil; Henry Grant, **CCBEU – Campinas**, Campinas, Brazil; Maria do Rosário, **CCBEU – Franca**, Franca, Brazil; Ane Cibele Palma, **CCBEU Inter Americano**, Curitiba, Brazil; Elen Flavia Penques da Costa, **Centro de Cultura Idiomas – Taubate**, Taubate, Brazil; Inara Lúcia Castillo Couto, **CEL LEP – São Paulo**, São Paulo, Brazil; Geysa de Azevedo Moreira, **Centro Cultural Brasil Estados Unidos (CCBEU Belém)**, Belém, Brazil; Sonia Patricia Cardoso, **Centro de Idiomas Universidad Manuela Beltrán**, Barrio Cedritos, Colombia; Geraldine Itiago Losada, **Centro Universitario Grupo Sol (Musali)**, Mexico City, Mexico; Nick Hilmers, **DePaul University**, Chicago, IL, USA; Monica L. Montemayor Menchaca, **EDIMSA**, Metepec, Mexico; Angela Whitby, **Edu-Idiomas Language School**, Cholula, Puebla, Mexico; Mary Segovia, **El Monte Rosemead Adult School**, Rosemead, CA, USA; Dr. Deborah Aldred, **ELS Language Centers, Middle East Region**, Abu Dhabi, United Arab Emirates; Leslie Lott, **Embassy CES**, Ft. Lauderdale, FL, USA; M. Martha Lengeling, **Escuela de Idiomas**, Guanajuato, Mexico; Pablo Frias, **Escuela de Idiomas UNAPEC**, Santo Domingo, Dominican Republic; Tracy Vanderhoek, **ESL Language Center**, Toronto, Canada; Kris Vicca and Michael McCollister, **Feng Chia University**, Taichung, Taiwan; Flávia Patricia do Nascimento Martins, **First Idiomas**, Sorocaba, Brazil; Andrea Taylor, **Florida State University in Panama**, Panamá, Panama; Carlos Lizárraga González, **Grupo Educativo Angloamericano**, Mexico City, Mexico; Dr. Martin Endley, **Hanyang University**, Seoul, Korea; Mauro Luiz Pinheiro, **IBEU Ceará**, Ceará, Brazil; Ana Lúcia da Costa Maia de Almeida, **IBEU Copacabana**, Copacabana, Brazil; Ana Lucia Almeida, Elisa Borges, **IBEU Rio**, Rio de Janeiro, Brazil; Maristela Silva, **ICBEU Manaus**, Manaus, Brazil; Magaly Mendes Lemos, **ICBEU São José dos Campos**, São José dos Campos, Brazil; Augusto Pelligrini Filho, **ICBEU São Luis**, São Luis, Brazil; Leonardo Mercado, **ICPNA**, Lima, Peru; Lucia Rangel Lugo, **Instituto Tecnológico de San Luis Potosí**, San Luis Potosí, Mexico; Maria Guadalupe Hernández Lozada, **Instituto Tecnológico de Tlalnepantla**, Tlalnepantla de Baz, Mexico; Greg Jankunis, **International Education Service**, Tokyo, Japan; Karen Stewart, **International House Veracruz**, Veracruz, Mexico; George Truscott, **Kinki University**, Osaka, Japan; Bo-Kyung Lee, **Hankuk University of Foreign Studies**, Seoul, Korea; Andy Burki, **Korea University, International Foreign Language School**, Seoul, Korea; Jinseo Noh, **Kwangwoon University**, Seoul, Korea; Nadezhda Nazarenko, **Lone Star College**, Houston, TX, USA; Carolyn Ho, **Lone Star College-Cy-Fair**, Cypress, TX, USA; Alice Ya-fen Chou, **National Taiwan University of Science and Technology**, Taipei, Taiwan; Gregory Hadley, **Niigata University of International and Information Studies, Department of Information Culture**, Niigata-shi, Japan; Raymond Dreyer, **Northern Essex Community College**, Lawrence, MA, USA; Mary Keter Terzian Megale, **One Way Línguas-Suzano**, São Paulo, Brazil; Jason Moser, **Osaka Shoin Joshi University**, Kashiba-shi, Japan; Bonnie Cheeseman, **Pasadena Community College** and **UCLA American Language Center**, Los Angeles, CA, USA; Simon Banha, **Phil Young's English School**, Curitiba, Brazil; Oh Jun Il, **Pukyong National University**, Busan, Korea; Carmen Gehrke, **Quatrum English Schools**, Porto Alegre, Brazil; Atsuko K. Yamazaki, **Shibaura Institute of Technology**, Saitama, Japan; Wen hsiang Su, **Shi Chien University, Kaohsiung Campus**, Kaohsiung, Taiwan; Richmond Stroupe, **Soka University, World Language Center**, Hachioji, Tokyo, Japan; Lynne Kim, **Sun Moon University (Institute for Language Education)**, Cheon An City, Chung Nam, Korea; Hiroko Nishikage, **Taisho University**, Tokyo, Japan; Diaña Peña Munoz and Zaira Kuri, **The Anglo**, Mexico City, Mexico; Alistair Campbell, **Tokyo University of Technology**, Tokyo, Japan; Song-won Kim, **TTI (Teacher's Training Institute)**, Seoul, Korea; Nancy Alarcón, **UNAM FES Zaragoza Language Center**, Mexico City, Mexico; Laura Emilia Fierro López, **Universidad Autónoma de Baja California**, Mexicali, Mexico; María del Rocío Domíngeuz Gaona, **Universidad Autónoma de Baja California**, Tijuana, Mexico; Saul Santos Garcia, **Universidad Autónoma de Nayarit**, Nayarit, Mexico; Christian Meléndez, **Universidad Católica de El Salvador**, San Salvador, El Salvador; Irasema Mora Pablo, **Universidad de Guanajuato**, Guanajuato, Mexico; Alberto Peto, **Universidad de Oxaca**, Tehuantepec, Mexico; Carolina Rodriguez Beltan, **Universidad Manuela Beltrán, Centro Colombo Americano**, and **Universidad Jorge Tadeo Lozano**, Bogotá, Colombia; Nidia Milena Molina Rodriguez, **Universidad Manuela Beltrán** and **Universidad Militar Nueva Granada**, Bogotá, Colombia; Yolima Perez Arias, **Universidad Nacional de Colombia**, Bogota, Colombia; Héctor Vázquez García, **Universidad Nacional Autónoma de Mexico**, Mexico City, Mexico; Pilar Barrera, **Universidad Técnica de Ambato**, Ambato, Ecuador; Deborah Hulston, **University of Regina**, Regina, Canada; Rebecca J. Shelton, **Valparaiso University, Interlink Language Center**, Valparaiso, IN, USA; Tae Lee, **Yonsei University**, Seodaemun-gu, Seoul, Korea; Claudia Thereza Nascimento Mendes, **York Language Institute**, Rio de Janeiro, Brazil; Jamila Jenny Hakam, **ELT Consultant**, Muscat, Oman; Stephanie Smith, **ELT Consultant**, Austin, TX, USA.

The authors would also like to thank the Four Corners editorial, production, and new media teams, as well as the Cambridge University Press staff and advisors around the world for their contributions and tireless commitment to quality.

Scope and sequence

LEVEL 2A	Learning outcomes	Grammar	Vocabulary
Welcome Unit Pages 2–3 **Classroom language** Page 4	**Students can . . .** ☑ ask questions about English words		Classroom instructions
Unit 1 Pages 5–14			
My interests A *I'm interested in fashion.* B *Can you repeat that, please?* C *Do you play sports?* D *Free time*	**Students can . . .** ☑ ask and talk about interests ☑ ask for repetition ☑ ask someone to speak more slowly ☑ ask and talk about sports and exercise habits ☑ talk about people's free-time activities	Present of *be* Simple present	Interests Sports and exercise
Unit 2 Pages 15–24			
Descriptions A *He's talkative and friendly.* B *I don't think so.* C *What do they look like?* D *People's profiles*	**Students can . . .** ☑ ask and talk about people's personalities ☑ say they think something is true and not true ☑ ask and talk about people's appearance ☑ describe their personality and appearance	*What . . . like?; be +* adjective (+ noun) *What . . . look like?;* order of adjectives	Personality adjectives Appearance
Unit 3 Pages 25–34			
Rain or shine A *It's extremely cold.* B *In my opinion, . . .* C *I'd like to play chess.* D *Where would you like to go?*	**Students can . . .** ☑ talk about the weather and seasons ☑ ask for and give an opinion ☑ talk about what they would like to do ☑ talk about a place they would like to visit	Adverbs of intensity; quantifiers with verbs *Would like* + infinitive	Weather Indoor activities
Unit 4 Pages 35–44			
Life at home A *There's a lot of light.* B *Can you turn down the music?* C *I always hang up my clothes!* D *What a home!*	**Students can . . .** ☑ ask and answer questions about their home ☑ make and agree to requests ☑ talk about household chores ☑ describe a home	*How many/much;* quantifiers before nouns Separable two-word phrasal verbs	Things in a home Household chores
Unit 5 Pages 45–54			
Health A *Breathe deeply.* B *I'm not feeling well.* C *How healthy are you?* D *Don't stress out!*	**Students can . . .** ☑ give and follow instructions ☑ say how they feel ☑ wish someone well ☑ ask and talk about healthy habits ☑ discuss ways to manage stress	Imperatives; adverbs of manner *How* questions	Parts of the body Healthy habits
Unit 6 Pages 55–64			
What's on TV? A *I love watching game shows.* B *I don't really agree.* C *I'm recording a documentary.* D *Popular TV*	**Students can . . .** ☑ talk about types of TV shows they like ☑ agree and disagree with an opinion ☑ describe future plans ☑ give their opinions about popular TV shows	Verb + infinitive or gerund Present continuous for future plans	Types of TV shows Television

v

Welcome

1 Working with a partner

A 🔊 Complete the conversations with the correct sentences. Then listen and check your answers.

- Can I borrow your pen?
- Let's compare our answers!
- Whose turn is it?
- Are you ready?

Not yet. Just a second.

1

Sure. Here you go.

2

What do you have for number one?

3

It's your turn.

4

B Pair work Practice the conversations.

2 Asking for help

A Match the questions and answers. Then practice with a partner.

1. How do you spell this word?   _d_   a. You say "welcome."
2. How do you pronounce this word?   _____   b. It means "not common."
3. What does this word mean?   _____   c. /ˈhɑbi/ (hobby).
4. How do you say _bienvenidos_ in English? _____   d. I-N-T-E-R-A-C-T-I-O-N-S.

B Write these four questions in the conversations. Then compare with a partner.

What does this word mean?	How do you say _Boa sorte_ in English?
How do you pronounce this word?	How do you spell your first name?

1. **A:** _____
   B: /ˈkantɛkst/ (context).
   A: Oh, that's easy!

2. **A:** _____
   B: I think it means "working together."
   A: Just like us!

3. **A:** _____
   B: E-M-I-K-O.
   A: That's a nice name.

4. **A:** _____
   B: You say "Good luck."
   A: I see. Well, good luck!

C 🔊 Listen and check your answers. Then practice the conversations with a partner.

3 Speaking Do you know?

A Pair work Think of two English words you know. Ask your partner about them.

   A: _What does the word_ kitten _mean?_
   B: _It means "baby cat."_

B Pair work Look at a page in the book and find two words. Write one word in each blank. Ask about the words.

How do you spell this word?   How do you pronounce this word?

_____   _____

C Group work Think of words or expressions you want to know in English. Ask your group how to say them. Can they answer?

   A: _How do you say_ _____ _in English?_
   B: _You say "_____ ."_

I can ask questions about English words.

3

Classroom language

A Write these actions below the correct pictures. Then compare with a partner.

Close your books.	Look at the picture.	Turn to page . . .
Listen.	✓ Open your books.	Work in groups.
Look at the board.	Raise your hand.	Work in pairs.

1. *Open your books.*

2. _____

3. _____

4. _____

5. _____

6. _____

7. _____

8. _____

9. _____

A: *What's number one?*
B: *It's . . .*

B 🔊 Listen and check your answers.

C 🔊 Listen to seven of the actions. Do each one.

4

My interests

LESSON A
- Interests
- Present of *be*

LESSON B
- Asking for repetition
- Asking someone to speak more slowly

LESSON C
- Sports and exercise
- Simple present

LESSON D
- Reading: "What's your hobby?"
- Writing: An interest

Warm-up

A Name the things in the picture. What do you think this person likes? Why?

B Do you like similar things?

I'm interested in fashion.

1 Vocabulary Interests

A 🔊 Match the words and the pictures. Then listen and check your answers.

a. art
b. fashion
c. languages
d. literature
e. politics
f. pop culture
g. sports
h. technology
i. travel

1. [d]
2.
3.
4.
5.
6.
7.
8.
9.

B Pair work Tell your partner about the things in Part A. Which ones do you love? like? hate?

2 Language in context Find new friends!

A 🔊 Read the survey. Then complete the survey with your own information.

Looking for new friends? *Find someone with similar interests!*

What's your name? _____	**Who's your favorite . . . ?**
Where are you from? _____	actor _____
How old are you? _____	actress _____
Are you single or married? _____	singer _____
Are you interested in . . . ?	**What's your favorite . . . ?**
travel yes / no	TV show _____
sports yes / no	movie _____
fashion yes / no	video game _____

B Group work Compare your information. Who are you similar to? How?

"Ming and I are similar. Our favorite movie is . . ."

3 Grammar 🔊   Present of *be*

Where **are** you from?	**Are** you interested in travel?
I**'m** from South Korea.	Yes, I **am**. No, I**'m not**.
How old **is** he?	**Is** he single?
He**'s** 22 years old.	Yes, he **is**. No, he**'s not**. / No, he **isn't**.
What **are** your friends' names?	**Are** they married?
Their names **are** Ming and Kathy.	Yes, they **are**. No, they**'re not**. / No, they **aren't**.

A Complete the conversations with the correct form of *be*. Then practice with
a partner.

1. **A:** What *'s* your name?

   B: Diego.

   A: Where _____ you from?

   B: Mexico City.

   A: _____ you single?

   B: No, I _____ not. I _____ married.

   A: _____ you interested in fashion?

   B: Not really. I _____ interested in sports.

2. **A:** Where _____ your parents from?

   B: My mother _____ from Osaka.

   A: _____ your father from Osaka, too?

   B: No, he _____ . He _____
   from Nagoya.

   A: What _____ they interested in?

   B: Art, languages, and literature.

   A: _____ they interested in travel?

   B: No, they _____ .

B Read the answers. Write the possible questions. Then compare with a partner.

1. *What are you interested in?*   Technology.
2. _____   I'm 20 years old.
3. _____   Johnny Depp.
4. _____   No, I'm from Seoul.
5. _____   Yes, I am.

C Pair work Ask and answer the questions in Part B.
Answer with your own information.

4 Speaking What are you interested in?

A Pair work Interview your partner. Take notes.

1. Are you interested in literature?	Yes.	Who's your favorite writer?
	No.	What books are in your house?
2. Are you interested in technology?	Yes.	What's a good cell phone?
	No.	How old is your cell phone?
3. Are you and your friends interested in similar things?	Yes.	What are you and your friends interested in?
	No.	What are your friends interested in?

B Pair work Tell another classmate about your partner's answers.

"Elena is interested in literature. Her favorite writer is Jane Austen."

5 Keep talking!

Go to page **125** for more practice.

    I can ask and talk about interests. ☑

B Can you repeat that, please?

1 Interactions   Asking for repetition

A Look at the pictures. Where are the people? What do you think they're talking about?

B 🔊 Listen to the conversations. Were your guesses from Part A correct? Then practice the conversations.

Fred: Fun party.
Carlos: Yeah, it is. Um, do you have the time?
Fred: It's . . . 9:50.
Carlos: I'm sorry. Can you repeat that, please?
Fred: Sure. It's 9:50.
Carlos: Wow! It's late.

Meg: So call me. OK?
Melissa: Sure. What's your number?
Meg: It's 629-555-0193.
Melissa: Can you say that more slowly, please?
Meg: Oh, sure. It's 629-555-0193.
Melissa: Got it. Thanks.

C 🔊 Listen to the expressions. Then practice the conversations again with the new expressions.

Asking for repetition

Can you repeat that, please?
Could you repeat that, please?
Could you say that again, please?

Asking someone to speak more slowly

Can you say that more slowly, please?
Could you say that more slowly, please?
Could you speak more slowly, please?

D Put the words in order. Then practice the questions with a partner.

1. you / can / that / please / repeat   _Can you repeat that, please?_
2. slowly / please / say / you / can / more / that   _____
3. again / could / say / you / that / please   _____
4. slowly / please / more / you / speak / could   _____

2 Pronunciation Intonation in *yes / no* and *Wh-* questions

A 🔊 Listen and repeat. Notice the intonation in *yes / no* and *Wh-* questions.

Do you have the time? ↗   Are you interested in fashion? ↗

Where are you from? ↘   What's your number? ↘

B 🔊 Listen and mark the intonation in the questions. Then practice with a partner.

1. Who's your favorite actress?   3. Are you from here?

2. Do you like parties?   4. What's your email address?

3 Listening Could you . . . ?

A 🔊 Listen to Clara's phone calls. Who does she talk to? Number the pictures from 1 to 3.

B 🔊 Listen again. Check (✓) the question Clara is going to ask at the end of each conversation.

1. ☐ Can you repeat that, please?   ☐ Can you say that more slowly, please?
2. ☐ Could you repeat that, please?   ☐ Could you say that more slowly, please?
3. ☐ Could you say that again, please?   ☐ Could you speak more slowly, please?

4 Speaking Class contact list

A Group work Ask four classmates their name, email address, and birthday. Make a list. Ask them to repeat or speak more slowly if necessary.

	Full name	Email address	Birthday
1.			
2.			
3.			
4.			

A: *What's your full name?*
B: *It's Maria Sanchez.*
A: *I'm sorry. Could you . . . ?*

B Share your information and create the class contact list.

I can ask for repetition. ☑
I can ask someone to speak more slowly. ☑

9

C Do you play sports?

1 Vocabulary Sports and exercise

A 🔊 Dan and Kathy are very active. Match the sentences and the pictures. Then listen and check your answers.

They . . .
bowl. _____
ski. _____
swim. _____

They play . . .
baseball. _____
golf. _____
table tennis. _____

They do . . .
gymnastics. _____
karate. _____
yoga. _____

B **Pair work** Which sports and exercises in Part A do you do? Tell your partner.

"I swim and play baseball."

2 Conversation A ski sale

A 🔊 Listen and practice.

Clerk: Can I help you?
Gina: Yes, thank you. I want something for my boyfriend. It's his birthday tomorrow.
Clerk: OK. What sports does he like? Does he play baseball?
Gina: No, he doesn't.
Clerk: How about table tennis? You can play together.
Gina: No, we don't really like table tennis.
Clerk: Well, does he ski?
Gina: Yes! He skis all the time. Do you sell skis?
Clerk: Yes, we do. And there's a ski sale right now.
Gina: Great!

Sporting Goods

B 🔊 Listen to a conversation between Gina and her boyfriend. Where are they?

3 Grammar 🔊 Simple present

What sports **do** you **like**?	**Do** you **sell** skis?
I **like** golf and karate.	Yes, I **do**. No, I **don't**.
I **don't like** basketball.	**Does** he **play** baseball?
What sports **does** he **play**?	Yes, he **does**. No, he **doesn't**.
He **plays** soccer.	**Do** they **like** table tennis?
He **doesn't play** baseball.	Yes, they **do**. No, they **don't**.
Where **do** they **do** yoga?	
They **do** yoga at home.	
They **don't do** yoga in the park.	

A Complete the paragraph with the simple present forms of the verbs. Then compare with a partner.

Every year, over a thousand men and women _____ (compete) in the Hawaii Ironman Triathlon. A triathlon _____ (have) three parts, but it _____ (not / have) three winners. The person with the best time for the three races _____ (win). They _____ (swim) for 3.86 km, _____ (bike) for 180 km, and then _____ (run) for 42.2 km. The winner _____ (get) $100,000.

B Put the words in order. Then ask and answer the questions. Answer with your own information.

1. soccer / do / play / on the weekend / you   _____
2. family / like / does / what sports / your   _____
3. best friend / your / where / does / exercise   _____
4. bowl / friends / do / your / on the weekend   _____

4 Speaking Do you . . . ?

A **Pair work** Complete the questions in the chart. Then interview your partner. Take notes.

1. Do you play sports on the weekend?	Yes. — What sports do you play?
	No. — What do you do on the weekend?
2. Do you watch sports on TV?	Yes. — What sports _____ ?
	No. — What _____ on TV?
3. Do you exercise in the morning?	Yes. — What _____ ?
	No. — When _____ ?

B **Pair work** Tell another classmate about your partner's answers.

"Ricardo plays basketball and does karate on the weekend."

5 Keep talking!

Go to page **126** for more practice.

I can ask and talk about sports and exercise habits. ☑

D Free time

1 Reading 🔊

A Look at the pictures. What is each person's hobby? Guess.

B Read the blog posts and check your guesses.

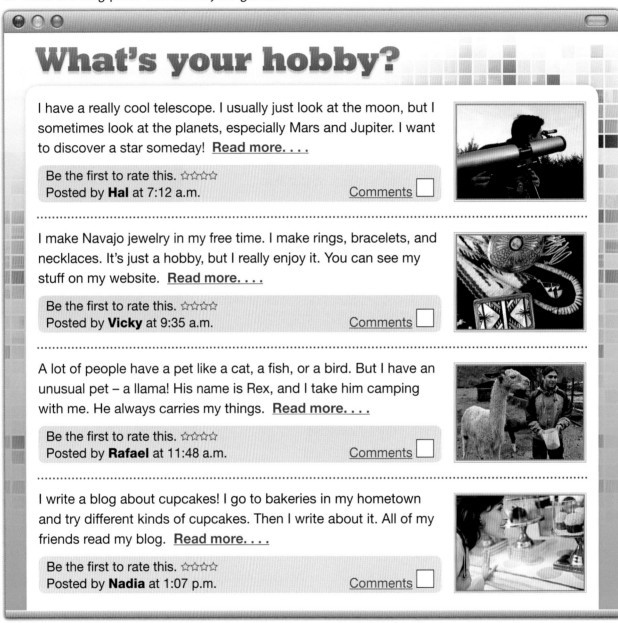

What's your hobby?

I have a really cool telescope. I usually just look at the moon, but I sometimes look at the planets, especially Mars and Jupiter. I want to discover a star someday! **Read more. . . .**

> Be the first to rate this. ☆☆☆☆☆
> Posted by **Hal** at 7:12 a.m.   Comments ☐

I make Navajo jewelry in my free time. I make rings, bracelets, and necklaces. It's just a hobby, but I really enjoy it. You can see my stuff on my website. **Read more. . . .**

> Be the first to rate this. ☆☆☆☆☆
> Posted by **Vicky** at 9:35 a.m.   Comments ☐

A lot of people have a pet like a cat, a fish, or a bird. But I have an unusual pet – a llama! His name is Rex, and I take him camping with me. He always carries my things. **Read more. . . .**

> Be the first to rate this. ☆☆☆☆☆
> Posted by **Rafael** at 11:48 a.m.   Comments ☐

I write a blog about cupcakes! I go to bakeries in my hometown and try different kinds of cupcakes. Then I write about it. All of my friends read my blog. **Read more. . . .**

> Be the first to rate this. ☆☆☆☆☆
> Posted by **Nadia** at 1:07 p.m.   Comments ☐

C Read the blog posts again. Which comment follows each post? Number the comments from 1 to 4.

1. Your stuff is great! Do you sell it?
2. So where's a good place to get one?
3. Good luck! Oh, what would you name it?
4. I love the picture. What does he eat?

D Pair work Rate each blog post and write a comment for one of the people. Discuss your ideas.

2 Listening Is that a fish?

A 🔊 Listen to John tell his friend about *gyotaku*. Number the pictures from 1 to 4.

B 🔊 Listen again. Answer the questions.

1. Where is *gyotaku* from? _____

2. Who does John work with? _____

3. Is it fun? _____

4. What does John sell? _____

3 Writing An interest

A Think of an interest you have. Answer the questions.

- What are you interested in?
- What do you do?
- What do you like about it?

B Write a blog post about an interest you have. Use the model and your answers in Part A to help you.

Collecting Autographs

I'm interested in autographs. I collect them from baseball players. Sometimes players write their names on pieces of paper. Sometimes they write on their photos. My favorite is an autographed baseball. It's just a hobby, but I really enjoy it.

C **Pair work** Share your writing. Ask and answer questions for more information.

4 Speaking Other people's interests

Group work Think about people you know. Which of the things below do they do? Ask and answer questions for more information.

writes a blog	wears cool clothes	has a favorite sports team
collects something	cooks a lot	makes something
travels a lot	has an unusual pet	reads a lot

A: *My friend Masao writes a blog.*
B: *What does he write about?*
A: *He usually writes about sports.*
C: *How often do you read it?*

I can talk about people's free-time activities.

Wrap-up

1 Quick pair review

Lesson A Brainstorm! Make a list of interests. How many do you know? You have one minute.

> fashion
>
> politics

Lesson B Do you remember? Check (✓) the questions you can ask when someone is speaking too fast or you want someone to repeat something. You have one minute.

✓ Could you repeat that, please?	____ Can I speak to Rita, please?
____ Can you say that more slowly, please?	____ Can you repeat that, please?
____ What does this mean?	____ Could you speak more slowly, please?
____ Could you say that again, please?	____ How do you spell that?

Lesson C Test your partner! Say the names of the sports and exercises. Can your partner say the correct verb? You have one minute.

Student A: Student B:

A: *Baseball.*
B: *Play baseball.*

Lesson D Guess! Describe or act out an interest or a sport, but don't say its name. Can your partner guess what it is? Take turns. You and your partner have two minutes.

A: *I write online every day. Other people read my writing.*
B: *Do you write a blog?*
A: *Yes, I do.*

2 In the real world

Who has unusual interests? Go online and find someone with one of these interests. Then write about it.

has an unusual pet	collects something
makes something	plays an unusual sport

> *Unusual Pets*
> *A woman in the U.S. has*
> *ducks as pets. . . .*

Descriptions

Warm-up

1

2

3

4

A Match the comments and the people in the pictures.

____ "We love your new sweater!"   ____ "That's very good. Good job!"

____ "What a great place!"   ____ "What's going to happen next?"

B What else can you say about the people in the pictures?

He's talkative and friendly.

1 Vocabulary Personality adjectives

A 🔊 Match the words and the pictures. Then listen and check your answers.

a. confident
b. creative
c. friendly
d. funny
e. generous
f. hardworking
g. serious
h. shy
i. talkative

1. g

2.

3.

4.

5.

6.

7.

8.

9.

B Pair work Which words describe you? Tell your partner.

"I'm hardworking and creative. Sometimes I'm shy."

2 Language in context Find an e-pal!

A 🔊 Read Nick's answers to an online form. Then complete the form with your own information.

Name
Nick Douglas
Hometown
Dallas, Texas
Age 18
What are your interests?
Fashion, literature, politics, movies, and sports
What are you like?
I'm talkative, friendly, and funny.

Name
Hometown
Age
What are your interests?
What are you like?

B Is Nick a good e-pal for you? Why or why not?

3 Grammar 🔊 *What . . . like?; be* + adjective (+ noun)

What are you like?	**What's she like?**	**What are they like?**
I'm talkative and friendly.	She's shy but friendly.	They're hardworking.
I'm **a** friendly and talkative **person**.	She's **a** shy but friendly **girl**.	They're hardworking **students**.

A Put the words in order. Then compare sentences with a partner.

1. teacher / a / Mrs. Jenkins / creative / is _____

2. Melissa / student / serious / a / is _____

3. funny / Bruno / is / talkative / and _____

4. are / Rodrigo and Miguel / confident / men _____

5. women / Marina and Elisa / are / hardworking _____

6. is / and / generous / Carrie / friendly _____

B Read the answers. Write the *What . . . like?* questions. Then practice with a partner.

1. *What are you like?* _____ I'm serious but friendly.
2. _____ Eva is a very funny girl.
3. _____ Matt and I are talkative people.
4. _____ Mr. and Mrs. Park are generous.
5. _____ I'm very serious and hardworking.
6. _____ His brother Sam is a creative guy.

4 Speaking He's hardworking.

A **Pair work** Choose three people from your family. Describe them to your partner.

brother	father	grandfather	husband
sister	mother	grandmother	wife

A: *My brother's name is Gi-woo.*
B: *What's he like?*
A: *Well, he's very hardworking. He's 26, and he's an accountant. He works late every day.*

B **Group work** Are the people you know similar or different?

A: *My brother is very hardworking.*
B: *Really? My mother is hardworking, too. She's a . . .*

5 Keep talking!

Go to page 127 for more practice.

I can ask and talk about people's personalities.	☑

B I don't think so.

1 Interactions — When you're not sure

A Look at the picture. Where are the people?

B 🔊 Listen to the conversation. Do Will and Joe know Mike well?
Then practice the conversation.

Will: What's your new roommate like?
Joe: Mike? Oh, he's nice, but he's not very talkative.
Will: Really? Is he shy?
Joe: I think so.

Will: Does he know many people here?
Joe: I don't think so.
Will: Well, maybe we can all go out together sometime.
Joe: That's a great idea.

C 🔊 Listen to the expressions. Then practice the conversation again with the new expressions.

Saying you think something is true	*Saying you think something isn't true*
I think so. I believe so. I guess so.	I don't think so. I don't believe so. I'm not really sure.

D Complete each response with one of the expressions from Part C. Then practice with a partner.

1. **A:** Is Rafael hardworking?   **B:** _____ He studies a lot.
2. **A:** Is Marilyn married?   **B:** _____ She doesn't have a ring.
3. **A:** Is David creative?   **B:** _____ He paints a lot.
4. **A:** Is Maria interested in travel? **B:** _____ She doesn't have a passport.
5. **A:** Is Sun-hee friendly?   **B:** _____ People like her.

2 Pronunciation *Is he* or *Is she*

A 🔊 Listen and repeat. Notice the pronunciation of *Is he* and *Is she*.

/ɪzi/

Is he hardworking?

/ɪʃi/

Is she a good student?

B 🔊 Listen and write *he* or *she*. Then practice with a partner.

1. Is _____ a creative person?
2. Is _____ your new roommate?
3. Is _____ a serious student?
4. Is _____ generous?

3 Listening People we know

A 🔊 Listen to two friends talk about different people. Who are they talking about? Check (✓) the correct answers.

1. ☐ a teacher
   ☐ a student
   ☐ a friend

2. ☐ a classmate
   ☐ a father
   ☐ a neighbor

3. ☐ best friends
   ☐ classmates
   ☐ teachers

B 🔊 Listen again. Circle the words you hear.

1. generous
   great
   funny
   creative

2. talkative
   hardworking
   shy
   friendly

3. serious
   confident
   nice
   talkative

4 Speaking Is he friendly?

A **Pair work** Talk about the people at the party. Use the words in the box and your own ideas.

friendly
talkative
shy
creative
serious
funny
single
married
a student
a teenager
a parent

Mike Teresa Allison Jun Toby George Carol

A: *Is Jun friendly?*
B: *I believe so.*
A: *Is he married?*
B: *I don't think so.*

B **Pair work** You want to meet one person at the party. Who do you talk to? Why?

I can say I think something is true and not true. ✓

What do they look like?

1 Vocabulary Appearance

A 🔊 Complete the descriptions with the correct words. Then listen and check your answers.

| bald | middle-aged | mustache | red | short | tall |

1. They're **young**. Rob is **short** and **overweight**, and May is _____ and **thin**. Rob has **straight brown hair**. May has **blond** hair. It's _____ and **wavy**.

2. They're _____ . Lou and Jill have **curly** _____ hair. Jill has **shoulder-length hair**. Lou has **little round glasses**.

3. They're **elderly**. They're **medium height**. Tony is _____ and has **a short white beard** and a _____ . Angela has **long gray** hair.

B **Pair work** Describe people in your family using the words in Part A.

"My brother is young. He's ten. My father has a mustache. And my . . ."

2 Conversation That's not my husband!

A 🔊 Listen and practice.

Waiter: Good evening. Can I help you?
Mrs. Gray: Yes, thank you. Is Ken Gray here? He's my husband.
Waiter: Mr. Gray? I don't know. What does he look like?
Mrs. Gray: He's tall, thin, and has black hair. And he has glasses.
Waiter: Does he have a mustache?
Mrs. Gray: Yes, he does.
Waiter: I think he's over there.
Mrs. Gray: No, that's not my husband! My husband has short hair.

B 🔊 Listen to the rest of the conversation. Who is Mr. Gray with?

3 Grammar 🔊 *What . . . look like?; order of adjectives*

What do you look like?	**What does he look like?**	**What do they look like?**
I'm short and overweight.	He's tall and thin.	They're middle-aged.
I have glasses.	He has a mustache.	They have curly red hair.

The order of adjectives is usually size, age, shape, and color.

She has **long gray** hair. (size + color)   He has **little round** glasses. (size + shape)

She has **new green** glasses. (age + color)   They have **curly red** hair. (shape + color)

A Look at the picture. Complete the sentences with two adjectives. Then compare with a partner.

big	brown	long	round	short	thin	wavy	young

1. He is a _____ and _____ man.
2. He has _____ hair.
3. He has a _____ beard.
4. He has _____ glasses.

B Put the words in order. Then ask and answer the questions.
Answer with your own information.

1. like / what / do / look / you _____
2. best friend / look / what / does / your / like _____
3. what / like / look / does / favorite singer / your _____

4 Speaking Who is it?

Pair work Describe a person in one of the pictures below, but don't say his or her name! Your partner guesses the person. Take turns.

Cara   Adam

Maggie   Lucy   Beth

Bo   Mei

Hai   Yi-Yin

"This person is tall and has short black hair."

5 Keep talking!

Student A go to page 128 and Student B go to page 130 for more practice.

I can ask and talk about people's appearance.

D People's profiles

1 Reading 🔊

A Read the webpage profiles. What is each person like?

ONLINE PROFILES

Name: Luc
Home: Montreal, Canada
Appearance: I'm tall and have long brown hair. I wear only black.
Personality: I'm a very creative person. I like to make different things from paper. I do it just for fun. I can make airplanes, birds, boats, and flowers.

Name: Bea
Home: London, U.K.
Appearance: I'm 60, with red hair. I always wear green glasses.
Personality: I think I'm a very generous person. I have a lot of free time, so I do a lot of volunteer work at local schools. To me, it's very important to give back to my community.

Name: Suchin
Home: Bangkok, Thailand
Appearance: I'm 30. I'm medium height, and I have short hair.
Personality: I'm friendly and hardworking. I work as a salesclerk in a clothing store. We sell clothing from northern Thailand there. In my free time, I play the *seung*, a traditional musical instrument.

Name: Marco
Home: Iquitos, Peru
Appearance: I'm tall and handsome, with long black hair.
Personality: I'm talkative and friendly. I have a part-time job. Iquitos is in the Amazon, so piranha fishing is very popular. I take tourists fishing, but we never keep the fish.

B Read the webpage again. Luc, Bea, Suchin, and Marco later uploaded these photos to their profiles. Write the name of the person under the correct photo.

_____   _____   _____   _____

C Who wrote each sentence? Write the names.

1. _____ But there's one problem – I can't swim!
2. _____ My neighbors complain about the noise.
3. _____ I especially like to work with children.
4. _____ I spend a lot of money on paper!

D **Pair work** Which person do you think is interesting? Why? Tell your partner.

2 Listening Starting a profile

A 🔊 Listen to Brian help his mother join a social networking site. Check (✓) the picture that Linda posts on the site.

B 🔊 Listen again. Check (✓) the information Brian's mother includes in her profile.

☐ Age ☐ Appearance ☐ Favorite actress ☐ Favorite singer ☐ Personality

3 Writing and speaking Guess who!

A Think about your appearance and your personality. Answer the questions.

- How old are you?
- What do you look like?
- What are you like?

B Write a description of yourself, but don't write your name! Use the model and your answers in Part A to help you.

> *Guess Who!*
> *I'm 18 years old. I'm thin and medium height. I have short black hair and glasses. I'm a friendly and talkative person, but sometimes I'm shy. I'm creative and very interested in art and fashion.*

C Group work Put your papers facedown on the table. Take one paper and read the description. Your group guesses who it is. Take turns.

A: *This person is interested in art and fashion.*
B: *I think I know. Is it Marta?*
A: *No, Marta has long hair. This person has short hair.*
B: *Oh, OK.*
C: *Is it . . . ?*

I can describe my personality and appearance. ☑

Wrap-up

1 Quick pair review

Lesson A **Brainstorm!** Make a list of personality adjectives. How many do you know? You have two minutes.

Lesson B **Test your partner!** Ask your partner the questions. Can your partner give the correct answers? You have one minute.

Student A: What are three ways to say you think something is true?

Student B: What are three ways to say you think something isn't true?

Lesson C **Do you remember?** Look at the picture.
Circle the correct word for each sentence. You have one minute.

1. This is Eduardo. He is **young** / **elderly**.
2. He has **short** / **long** gray hair.
3. His hair is **straight** / **curly**.
4. He has **little** / **big** glasses.
5. He has a **mustache** / **beard**.

Lesson D **Find out!** Are any of your and your partner's friends similar? Take turns. You and your partner have two minutes.

A: *My friend is tall and has long black hair. She's very funny.*
B: *My friend is tall and has long black hair. She's funny, too!*

2 In the real world

Who are you like? Go online and find a musician, an actor, or an actress who is similar to you. Then write a description of him or her.

- What does he or she look like?
- What is he or she like?

> *Scarlett Johansson*
> *Scarlett Johansson is similar*
> *to me. She is medium height.*
> *She has long hair. . . .*

Rain or shine

Warm-up

A Describe the pictures. Where are the people? What are they doing?

B Do you ever do these activities? When do you do them?

A *It's extremely cold.*

1 Vocabulary Weather

A 🔊 Label the pictures with the correct words. Then listen and check your answers.

Weather				
cloudy	rainy	snowy	sunny	windy

Temperature			
cold	cool	hot	warm

← 6. _____

← 7. _____

← 8. _____

← 9. _____

1. _____ 2. _____ 3. _____ 4. _____ 5. _____

B Pair work What's the weather like in your country in each season? Complete the chart with the words from Part A. Then compare answers.

spring	summer	fall	winter		rainy season	dry season

2 Language in context Favorite seasons

A 🔊 Listen to people talk about their favorite season. Which places are cool?

My favorite season is spring. It's fairly cool, and it rains quite a bit, but it's a good time to see flowers.
– Jan, Lisse, Holland

I like summer a lot. It's very windy – great for windsurfing! And it doesn't rain at all then.
– Fouad, Essaouira, Morocco

Fall is my favorite. It's sunny and cool, and in late October, 150 million butterflies arrive!
– Juan, Morelia, Mexico

I love winter. It's extremely cold and it snows a lot, but that's when the Sapporo Snow Festival is.
– Rie, Sapporo, Japan

B What about you? What's your favorite season? What's the weather like then?

3 Grammar 🔊 Adverbs of intensity; quantifiers with verbs

Adverbs of intensity	Quantifiers with verbs
It's **extremely** cold.	It snows **a lot**.
It's **very** windy.	It rains **quite a bit**.
It's **really** hot.	It snows **a little**.
It's **pretty** sunny.	It does**n't** rain **very much**.
It's **fairly** cool.	It does**n't** rain **at all**.
It's **somewhat** cloudy.	

Add the adverbs and quantifiers to the sentences. Then compare with a partner.

1. It snows in Moscow in the winter. (a lot) *It snows a lot in Moscow in the winter.*
2. It rains in Seattle in the winter. (quite a bit) _____
3. It's cold in Busan in January. (extremely) _____
4. It's cool in Rabat in the rainy season. (fairly) _____
5. It snows in Lima in July. (not . . . at all) _____
6. It's windy in Wellington all year. (pretty) _____

4 Listening Think about the weather!

A 🔊 Listen to people talk about the weather in three cities. Which city is one of the people planning to visit? Circle the city.

1. Istanbul, Turkey   It's _____ cold in the winter.
2. Antigua, Guatemala   The _____ season is from November to April.
3. Beijing, China   It's _____ and _____ in the spring.

B 🔊 Listen again. Complete the sentences with the correct words.

5 Speaking True or false?

A Write two true sentences and two false sentences about the weather where you live. Use these words and expressions.

pretty sunny	rain a lot	somewhat cloudy
extremely hot	very windy	fairly cool
really cold	snow	

B Pair work Read your sentences. Your partner corrects the false sentences. Take turns.

> **A:** *It's pretty sunny in the winter.*
> **B:** *I think that's false. It's pretty cloudy in the winter.*

6 Keep talking!

Student A go to page 129 and Student B go to page 131 for more practice.

I can talk about the weather and seasons.

B *In my opinion, . . .*

1 Interactions   Opinions

A Do you ever make phone calls over the Internet? What do you like about it? What don't you like?

B 🔊 Listen to the conversation. Where are the three people? Then practice the conversation.

Cindy: So, Luk, how are things in Bangkok?
Luk: Great. It's warm and sunny today.
Brian: It's really cold here in Chicago. So when are you coming to see us?
Luk: Well, when's a good time to visit?
Cindy: Hmm . . . I'm not sure.
Luk: Brian? What do you think?

Brian: I think fall is a good time. The weather is great, and there's a lot to do.
Cindy: Yeah, we can all go to a baseball game then.
Luk: That would be great!

C 🔊 Listen to the expressions. Then practice the conversation again with the new expressions.

Asking for an opinion	Giving an opinion
What do you think? What are your thoughts? What's your opinion?	I think . . . I'd say . . . In my opinion, . . .

D Number the sentences from 1 to 6. Then compare with a partner.

_____ **A:** Well . . . what's your favorite season?

_1_ **A:** When are you going to New York?

_____ **A:** I think spring is a great time to visit. It's usually warm and sunny then.

_____ **B:** I don't know. What do you think? When's a good time to visit?

_____ **B:** Really? OK. Maybe we'll go to New York in May.

_____ **B:** My favorite season is spring.

2 **Listening** When's a good time to visit?

A 🔊 Listen to three people talk to friends about a good time to visit these cities. Are their friends' opinions the same or different? Circle your answers.

Rio de Janeiro, Brazil

Queenstown, New Zealand

Marseille, France

1. the same / different   2. the same / different   3. the same / different

B 🔊 Listen again. Write T (true) or F (false) next to the sentences.

1. Gabriel is from Rio de Janeiro, but Bianca isn't. __F__

2. It's very hot in Rio de Janeiro in February. _____

3. Patricia thinks it's fine to visit New Zealand anytime. _____

4. It's extremely cold in New Zealand in July and August. _____

5. Sophie is from Marseille. _____

6. A lot of stores and restaurants in France close in August. _____

3 **Speaking** Good time, bad time

A Pair work Discuss the weather and seasons where you live. Give your opinions.

- When's a good season to visit?
- What months are especially good?
- What's the weather like then?
- What kinds of things do people do then?
- When's not a good time to visit? Why not?

> **A:** *I think spring is a good season to visit. What do you think?*
> **B:** *Yes, I'd say May is good.*
> **A:** *The weather is warm then.*
> **B:** *And there are some great festivals.*

B Group work Share your opinions with another pair. Do you have the same opinions?

I can ask for and give an opinion. ☑

C I'd like to play chess.

1 Vocabulary Indoor activities

A 🔊 Complete the phrases with the correct words. Then listen and check your answers.

a board game	cookies	a jigsaw puzzle	popcorn
chess	a crossword	a nap	a video

a. bake _____

b. do _____

c. do _____

d. make _____

e. make _____

f. play _____

g. play _____

h. take _____

B Pair work Rank these activities from 1 (fun) to 8 (not fun at all). Then compare answers.

> **A:** I do a crossword every day, so I think that's really fun. How about you?
> **B:** I never take a nap. I don't think that's fun at all. It's my number eight.

2 Conversation It's raining!

A 🔊 Listen and practice.

Joanie: Oh, no! It's raining!
Evan: We can't go on our picnic.
Joanie: No. So, what would you like to do?
Would you like to do a jigsaw puzzle?
Evan: Not really. Would you like to play chess?
Joanie: Um, yeah, I would.
Evan: We can make some popcorn, too.
Joanie: Great idea. But let's play a little later.
Evan: OK. Why?
Joanie: I'd like to take a short nap.

B 🔊 Listen to their conversation later in the day. What does Evan want to do?

3 Grammar 🔊 *Would like + infinitive*

What **would** you **like to do**?
   I'd like to play chess.
Where **would** he **like to play** chess?
   He**'d like to play** right here.
	Would you **like to do** a jigsaw puzzle?
	   Yes, I **would**. No, I **wouldn't**.
	Would they **like to take** a nap?
	   Yes, they **would**. No, they **wouldn't**.

A Circle the correct words. Then practice with a partner.

1. **A:** Which game would you like **play / to play**?

   B: **I'd like to / I would to** play chess.

2. **A:** Would you like **do / to do** a crossword now?

   B: No, **I'd not / I wouldn't**. I don't like crosswords.

3. **A:** What **do / would** you like to do tonight?

   B: **I'd like / I would** to watch TV with my friends.

B **Pair work** Make true sentences with *I'd like to* or *I wouldn't like to*.
Tell your partner.

have class outside	play chess after class	stay in this weekend	take a nap right now

4 Pronunciation Reduction of *would you*

A 🔊 Listen and repeat. Notice how *would you* is pronounced /wʊdʒə/.

Would you like to play a board game?   Which game **would you** like to play?

B **Pair work** Practice the questions in Exercise 3A again. Reduce *would you* to /wʊdʒə/.

5 Speaking I'd like to . . .

A **Pair work** Look out these windows and describe the weather. Then decide what you'd like to do together on each day. Take notes.

1.   2.   3.

   A: *It's cool and rainy today. What would you like to do?*
   B: *I'd like to do a jigsaw puzzle. How about you?*

B **Group work** Share your ideas with another pair. Ask and answer questions for more information.

6 Keep talking!

Go to page 132 for more practice.

> **I can** talk about what I would like to do. ☑

D *Where would you like to go?*

1 Reading ◄))

A Read the article. Where do you think it is from? Check (✓) the correct answer.

☐ a vacation blog   ☐ a tourist brochure   ☐ a textbook   ☐ a weather report

CANADA THROUGH THE SEASONS

The weather is very different in this large country, so there's something to do for everyone in every season.

Arctic Circle
British Columbia
Pacific Ocean
Alberta
Churchill
Hudson Bay
Calgary
Manitoba
Quebec
Victoria
Saskatchewan
Ontario
the United States
Toronto
Atlantic Ocean

Spring can arrive in February in Victoria on the west coast. In other parts of Canada, it gets warm in early April, and spring weather continues until June. In British Columbia, you can kayak, camp, or take a train trip through the Rocky Mountains.

Summer brings warm to hot weather from May to September. This is a great time to fish in one of Canada's many lakes; kayak among whales in Churchill, Manitoba; or have some Wild West fun at the Calgary Stampede.

Fall brings cool temperatures in September and October. It's a good time of year to see the fall leaves in eastern Canada, enjoy hiking, visit museums, or go to the Toronto International Film Festival.

Snow begins to fall in November, and temperatures drop. Days are short in winter, but you can ski, go to an ice festival, or see the northern lights. In parts of British Columbia, the snow doesn't stay long and you can golf all year!

B Read the article again. When can you use these things? Write the season.

_____   _____   _____   _____

C **Group work** Imagine you can visit Canada. When and where would you go? Why? Discuss your ideas.

2 Writing An email to a friend

A Think of a place and a friend you would like to visit. Answer the questions.

- What is your friend's name?
- Where does your friend live?
- When do you plan to visit?
- What would you like to do there?

B Write an email to a friend about your travel plans. Use the model and your answers in Part A to help you.

| Kate Spencer to Hee-jin Choi | Send |

Hi Hee-jin,

I have good news. I can visit you in Seoul this summer!

Tell me about Seoul. What's the weather like in the summer? Is it really hot?

As you know, I'm very interested in art and food. So I'd like to visit the National Museum and go to some really good restaurants. What about you? What would you like to do?

This is so exciting! See you soon.

Kate

C **Pair work** Share your writing. Ask and answer questions for more information.

3 Speaking A place I'd like to visit

A Think about a place you'd like to visit in your own country or a different country. Take notes.

Place: _____		
When would you like to go?	Why would you like to go then?	What would you like to do there?

B **Group work** Share your ideas. Ask and answer questions for more information.

A: *I'd really like to go to Kyoto in the spring.*
B: *Why would you like to go then?*
A: *Because I'd like to see the cherry blossoms.*
C: *What else would you like to do there?*

I can talk about a place I would like to visit.

Wrap-up

1 Quick pair review

Lesson A **Brainstorm!** Make a list of words for weather and words for temperature. How many do you know? You have two minutes.

Lesson B **Do you remember?** Check (✓) the questions you can ask when you want someone's opinion. You have one minute.

☐ What's your opinion?

☐ What's your teacher's name?

☐ What's the weather like today?

☐ What are your thoughts?

☐ What are you like?

☐ What do you think?

Lesson C **Find out!** What is one thing both you and your partner would like to do outside this weekend? What is one thing you both would like to do inside? Take turns. You and your partner have two minutes.

A: *I'd like to play chess inside. Would you?*
B: *No. I'd like to bake cookies. Would you?*
A: *Yes, I would.*

Lesson D **Guess!** Describe a famous place in your country, but don't say its name. Can your partner guess where it is? Take turns. You and your partner have two minutes.

A: *It's hot, and it's a big city. People have parties on the beach.*
B: *Is it Rio de Janeiro?*
A: *Yes, it is.*

2 In the real world

Where would you like to go? Go online and find the typical weather for that place in every season. Then write about it.

> *Chicago*
> *I'd like to go to Chicago. There are four seasons. It's extremely cold in the winter. It's very windy in the spring. . . .*

Life at home

Warm-up

a. ☐

b. ☐

c. ☐

d. ☐

A These are the homes of world leaders. Match the countries and the pictures. Check your answers on page 44.

_____ Brazil   _____ France   _____ Iceland   _____ Japan

B Rank the homes you would like to visit from 1 (really want to visit) to 4 (don't want to visit).

A There's a lot of light.

1 Vocabulary Things in a home

A 🔊 Label the pictures with the correct words. Then listen and check your answers.

| bathtub | bed | coffee table | refrigerator |

c. shower

a. sink

b. toilet

d. _____

bathroom

a. curtains

c. closet

b. dresser

d. _____

bedroom

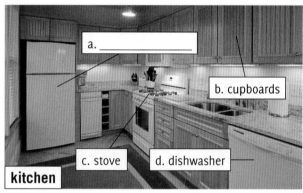

a. _____

b. cupboards

c. stove   d. dishwasher

kitchen

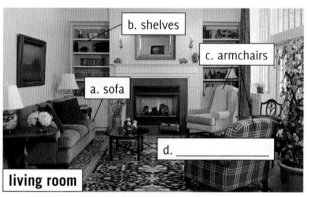

b. shelves

c. armchairs

a. sofa

d. _____

living room

B **Pair work** Which of the things in Part A do you have in your home? Tell your partner.

2 Language in context A new apartment

A 🔊 Listen to the conversation. Beth has a new apartment. Which room does Lori like?

Lori: Your new place is nice! How many rooms are there?

Beth: There are four – a kitchen, a living room, a bathroom, and a bedroom.

Lori: I really like your kitchen.

Beth: Thanks. There aren't many cupboards, and there isn't much space, but that's OK. I hardly ever cook.

Lori: Look at all the windows in your living room!

Beth: Yeah, there's a lot of light in here. But . . . there's also a lot of noise!

B What about you? What is important to you when you move into a new house or apartment?

3 Grammar 🔊 *How many/much; quantifiers before nouns*

How many cupboards are there?

There are	a lot of some a few	cupboards.
There are**n't**	many any	cupboards.

How much light is there?

There's	a lot of some a little	light.
There is**n't**	much any	light.

A Complete the questions with *many* or *much*. Answer the questions about the home in Exercise 1. Then practice with a partner.

1. How _____ space is there in the kitchen? _____
2. Are there _____ cupboards in the kitchen? _____
3. How _____ chairs are there in the living room? _____
4. Are there _____ shelves in the bathroom? _____
5. How _____ light is there in the bedroom? _____

B Pair work Ask and answer questions about the apartment in Exercise 2.

rooms / apartment cupboards / kitchen space / kitchen
light / living room windows / living room noise / apartment

> **A:** *How many rooms are there in the apartment?*
> **B:** *There are four rooms. Are there many cupboards in the kitchen?*

4 Speaking My home

Pair work Add three questions below. Then interview your partner. Find out three things that are similar about your homes.

- Do you live in a house or an apartment?
- How many rooms are there?
- Are there many closets in the bedroom?
- Is there much space in the bathroom?

_____
_____
_____

> **A:** *Do you live in a house or an apartment?*
> **B:** *I live in a small apartment.*
> **A:** *Me, too.*

house

apartment

5 Keep talking!

Go to page 133 for more practice.

I can ask and answer questions about my home. ✓

B Can you turn down the music?

1 Interactions | Requests

A What are your neighbors like? Do you like them?

B 🔊 Listen to the conversation. Why does Keisha call her neighbor? Then practice the conversation.

Carlos: Hello?
Keisha: Hi. It's Keisha from downstairs. Are you having a party?
Carlos: Uh-huh. Are we being noisy?
Keisha: I'm afraid so. Can you turn down the music, please?

Carlos: Sure. I can do it now.
Keisha: Thank you. I have an exam tomorrow, and I'm trying to study.
Carlos: I understand.
Keisha: Thanks again.

C 🔊 Listen to the expressions. Then practice the conversation again with the new expressions.

Making a request

Can you turn down the music, please?
Could you turn down the music, please?
Would you turn down the music, please?

Agreeing to a request

Sure.
No problem.
I'd be happy to.

D Match the requests and the responses. Then practice with a partner.

1. Can you turn down your TV, please?
2. Can you move your car, please?
3. Could you answer the phone, please?
4. Would you open the curtains, please?

a. I'd be happy to. I'm going to work now, anyway.
b. Sure. I think it's for me.
c. No problem. Sorry about the noise.
d. Sure. There isn't much light in here.

2 **Pronunciation** Intonation in requests

A 🔊 Listen and repeat. Notice the falling intonation in these requests.

Can you turn down the music, please?   Can you move your car, please?

B Pair work Practice the questions in Exercise 1D again. Pay attention to your intonation.

3 **Listening** Friendly requests

A 🔊 Listen to three people call their neighbors. Where does each caller live? Circle the correct answers.

1. apartment / house   2. apartment / house   3. apartment / house

B 🔊 Listen again. What does each caller want the neighbor to do? Check (✓) the correct answers.

1. ☐ stop the party   2. ☐ get the cat   3. ☐ stop exercising
   ☐ turn down the TV   ☐ move the car   ☐ exercise earlier
   ☐ turn down the music   ☐ buy some milk   ☐ stop the party

4 **Speaking** Neighbor to neighbor

A Match the requests and the problems.

1. Can you move it, please?   3. Could you come and get it, please?
2. Could you put it in the garbage can, please?   4. Would you turn it down, please?

Your neighbor's cat is at your door.   Your neighbor's TV is very noisy.   Your neighbor's car is in your parking space.   Your neighbor's garbage isn't in the garbage can.

B Pair work Call your neighbor. Identify yourself and explain the situation. Make a request. Take turns.

   A: *Hello.*
   B: *Hi. It's Mike from downstairs. Your cat is at my door.*
      Could you come and get it, please?
   A: *Sure. I'd be happy to.*

C Pair work Think of two more requests. Then call your partner to make the requests. Take turns.

I can make and agree to requests. ☑

I always hang up my clothes!

1 Vocabulary Household chores

A 🔊 Label the pictures with the correct words. Then listen and check your answers.

clean out the closet	drop off the dry cleaning	pick up the magazines	take out the garbage
clean up the yard	hang up the clothes	put away the dishes	wipe off the counter

1. _____   2. _____   3. _____   4. _____

5. _____   6. _____   7. _____   8. _____

B Pair work Which chores in Part A do you do? Tell your partner.

"I always clean up the yard on the weekend. I also drop off the dry cleaning."

2 Conversation Let's clean it up!

A 🔊 Listen and practice.

Ken: This place is a mess. Let's clean it up before Mom and Dad get home.

Paul: Good idea. Well, I can put the dishes away and wipe off the counter.

Ken: And the garbage is full. Could you take it out?

Paul: Sure. No problem.

Ken: And you know, your bedroom is a mess, too. Your clothes are all over the floor. Would you pick them up, please?

Paul: Yeah, I guess.

Ken: And then hang them up in the closet?

Paul: OK, but what are *you* going to do?

B 🔊 Listen to the rest of the conversation. Which chore is Ken going to do?

3 Grammar 🔊 Separable two-word phrasal verbs

I **take out** the garbage.	Could you **hang up** your clothes, please?
I **take** the garbage **out**.	Could you **hang** your clothes **up**, please?
I **take** it **out**.	Could you **hang** them **up**, please?
Not: ~~I take out it.~~	*Not:* ~~Could you hang up them, please?~~

A Rewrite the sentences. Then compare with a partner.

1. Let's hang up the dry cleaning.   *Let's hang the dry cleaning up.*

2. Could you put away your clothes, please?   _____

3. How often do you take out the garbage?   _____

4. I clean out my closets once a year.   _____

B Complete the sentences with the correct verbs. Use either *it* or *them*. Then compare with a partner.

clean out	drop off	pick up	take out
✓clean up	hang up	put away	wipe off

1. The living room is a mess. Let's *clean it up*_____ before the party.

2. Why is your coat on the chair? Can you _____ in the closet?

3. The garbage is full. Could you _____ right away, please?

4. This closet is full of old clothes and books. Let's _____ .

5. The dishes are in the dishwasher. Would you _____ for me?

6. This table isn't clean. Can you _____ before dinner, please?

7. These books belong to the library. Could you _____ for me?

8. Your magazines are all over the floor. Would you _____ , please?

4 Speaking What a chore!

A Pair work Interview your partner. Check (✓) his or her answers.

How often do you . . . ?	My partner
1. put away the dishes	
2. clean up your bedroom	
3. take out the garbage	
4. clean out your closet	
5. hang up your clothes	

B Group work Tell your group about your partner's answers. Who does a lot of chores? Who doesn't?

"Daniel does a lot of chores. He puts away the dishes and takes out the garbage every day."

5 Keep talking!

Go to page **134** for more practice.

I can talk about household chores.

41

D What a home!

1 Reading ◀))

A Look at the pictures. Describe each home.

B Read the article. Check (✓) the best title for the article.

☐ Crazy Houses in the United States   ☐ Daily Life in a Strange House

☐ Unusual Houses from Around the World   ☐ How to Build Your Dream Home

The Storybook House

The classic children's story "Hansel and Gretel" inspired this unusual home in the U.S. The owners built the house by hand and included five fireplaces inside.

The Shoe House

This house in the U.S. has a living room, two bathrooms, a kitchen, and three bedrooms. There's even a shoe mailbox. The owner had a few shoe stores. No one lives there now, but there are tours of the house.

The Crazy House

People in Vietnam call this house the Crazy House because it looks strange. Part of the house is a tree, and it has unusual twists and turns. You can also see big animals on the outside. The house is a hotel and a tourist attraction.

The Upside-down House

In this house in Poland, the furniture hangs from the ceiling! No one lives there, but it's a popular tourist attraction. It took the workers a long time to build the house. They often felt sick inside.

C Read the article again. Answer the questions.

1. How did the owners build the Storybook House? _____

2. How many rooms are there in the Shoe House? _____

3. What can you see on the outside of the Crazy House? _____

4. What is unusual about the inside of the Upside-down House? _____

D **Pair work** Which house would you like to stay in? Why? Tell your partner.

2 Listening A tour of Graceland

A Graceland was Elvis Presley's home in Memphis, Tennessee. Look at the pictures in Part B of four rooms in the home. What do you see? What do you think the house is like?

B 🔊 Listen to Sam and Haley take a tour of Graceland. Number the rooms from 1 to 4.

TV room

kitchen

dining room

living room

C 🔊 Listen again. What is each person's favorite room? Complete the sentences.

1. Sam's favorite room is the _____ .
2. Haley's favorite room is the _____ .

3 Writing and speaking Dream home

A Imagine your dream home. Answer the questions.

- Where is your dream home?
- How many rooms does it have?
- What does it look like?
- Is there anything unusual about your home?

B Write a description of your dream home. Use the model and your answers in Part A to help you.

C Pair work Share your writing. Ask and answer questions for more information.

A: *What color is the house?*
B: *It's white.*
A: *What is your favorite part of the house?*
B: *The swimming pool.*

My Dream Home
My dream home is on the beach in Hawaii. It's a very big house. It has five bedrooms, five bathrooms, and a lot of light and space. There are two kitchens. One kitchen is inside the house. The other kitchen is outside because we have a lot of barbecues on the beach!

I can describe a home. ✓

Wrap-up

1 Quick pair review

Lesson A **Brainstorm!** Make a list of rooms in a house and the things that go in each room. How many do you know? You have two minutes.

Lesson B **Do you remember?** Complete the conversations with the correct words. You have two minutes.

1. **A:** C_ould_____ you turn down the music, please?
   B: No p_____ .
2. **A:** W_____ you answer the phone, please?
   B: I'd be h_____ to.
3. **A:** Could buy some milk, p_____ ?
   B: S_____ .

Lesson C **Test your partner!** Act out a chore. Can your partner guess what it is? Take turns. You and your partner have two minutes.

Lesson D **Guess!** Describe a room in your house, but don't say its name. Can your partner guess what room it is? Take turns. You and your partner have two minutes.

A: *This is my favorite room. There are three posters on the wall.*
B: *Is it your bedroom?*
A: *Yes, it is.*

2 In the real world

Go online and find information in English about an unusual house. Then write about it.

- Why is it unusual?
- What are the rooms like?
- Find a picture of the home, if possible.

> *An Unusual Home*
> *The House on the Rock has many interesting rooms. One room is 218 feet long and has 3,264 windows.*

Answers to Warm-up, Part A (page 35)
a. Japan b. Iceland c. Brazil d. France

Health

LESSON A
- Parts of the body
- Imperatives; adverbs of manner

LESSON B
- Saying how you feel
- Wishing someone well

LESSON C
- Healthy habits
- *How* questions

LESSON D
- Reading: "Feeling Stressed?"
- Writing: Managing stress

Warm-up

A Describe the picture. Which activities are good for you? Which ones aren't?

B Do you ever do any of the things in the picture? Which ones?

A Breathe deeply.

1 Vocabulary Parts of the body

A 🔊 Label the pictures with the correct words. Then listen and check your answers.

a. arm	d. finger	g. head	j. mouth	m. shoulder
b. ear	e. foot (feet)	h. knee	k. neck	n. stomach
c. eye	f. hand	i. leg	l. nose	o. wrist

1.

2. **tooth (teeth)**

3.

4.

5.

6. **back**

7.

8.

1.

9.

10.

11. **throat**

12.

13.

2.

14.

15.

16.

17.

18.

19. **ankle**

20. **toe**

3.

B Pair work Point to a part of your body. Your partner names it. Take turns.

"That's your arm. And those are your ears."

2 Language in context Yoga for beginners

A 🔊 Match the exercises with the yoga pictures in Exercise 1. Listen and check your answers.

A. _____ Place your right foot carefully on your left leg. Stretch your arms over your head. Hold for 30 seconds. Lower your arms and foot slowly.

B. _____ Repeat on the other side. Place your left foot carefully on your right leg. Stretch your arms over your head. Hold for 30 seconds.

C. _____ Stand up. Hold your stomach in. Keep your back and neck straight. Relax your arms. Don't hold your breath. Breathe slowly and deeply.

B What about you? Do you do yoga? If not, would you like to try it? Why or why not?

3 Grammar 🔊 | Imperatives; adverbs of manner

Breathe slowly and deeply.
Stretch your arms.
Hold for 30 seconds.
Repeat on the other side.

Don't breathe quickly.
Don't relax your arms.
Don't hold your breath.
Don't repeat on the other side.

Adjective	Adverb
slow	slow**ly**
careful	careful**ly**
deep	deep**ly**
noisy	nois**ily**

A Complete these exercise tips with the correct imperative form. Then compare with a partner.

✓do	drink	eat	exercise	find	stretch

1. _Don't do_____ too much the first day!
2. _____ your body for a few minutes.
3. _____ a place with a lot of space.

4. _____ some water.
5. _____ a big meal before you exercise.
6. _____ twice a week.

B Circle the correct adverbs. Then compare with a partner.

1. Walk **quickly / slowly** for 20 minutes every day.
2. Eat **quickly / slowly** at every meal.
3. Breathe **heavily / deeply** when you exercise.
4. Sit **quietly / noisily** for a few minutes each day.
5. Stretch **carefully / heavily** every morning.

4 Pronunciation Reduction of *and*

🔊 Listen and repeat. Notice how *and* is pronounced /ən/ before some consonant sounds.

　　　　　　　/ən/　　　　　　　　　　　　/ən/
Breathe slowly and deeply.　　Keep your back and neck straight.

5 Speaking Lower your arms slowly.

Pair work Make sentences with the words below.
Your partner does the actions. Take turns.

"Point to your nose slowly."

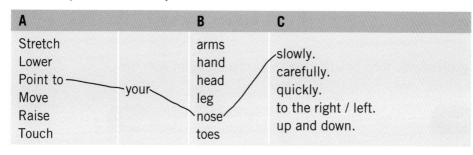

A	B	C
Stretch	arms	slowly.
Lower	hand	carefully.
Point to	head	quickly.
Move	your leg	to the right / left.
Raise	nose	up and down.
Touch	toes	

6 Keep talking!
Go to page **135** for more practice.

I can give and follow instructions. ☑

B *I'm not feeling well.*

1 Health problems

🔊 Listen. Then act out a health problem. Your partner guesses it.

 a backache

 a cold

 a cough

 an earache

 a fever

 the flu

 a headache

 a sore throat

 a stomachache

 a toothache

"Do you have a cold?"

2 Interactions   When you're not feeling well

A 🔊 Listen to the conversation. What's wrong with Margaret?
Then practice the conversation.

Debbie: Hey, Margaret. How are you?
Margaret: I'm not feeling well.
Debbie: Oh? What's wrong?

Margaret: I have a headache. I think I'd
like to go home and rest.
Debbie: That's fine. Take it easy.

B 🔊 Listen to the expressions. Then practice the conversation again with the
new expressions.

Saying how you feel
I'm not feeling well.
I don't feel so good.
I feel awful.

Wishing someone well
Take it easy.
Get well soon.
I hope you feel better.

3 Listening What's wrong?

A 🔊 Listen to four phone conversations. Number the pictures from 1 to 4.

B 🔊 Listen again. How does each caller wish the person well? Write the expression.

1. _____   3. _____
2. _____   4. _____

4 Speaking We're not feeling well.

Class activity Role-play these situations. Then change roles.

Group A: Walk around the class and ask people in Group B how they feel. Use expressions from Exercise 2.

Group B: Imagine you have a health problem. Tell the people in Group A about it. Use expressions from Exercise 2.

A: *How are you?*
B: *I don't feel so good.*
A: *Oh? What's wrong?*
B: *I have a stomachache.*
A: *I'm sorry to hear that. I hope you feel better.*

I can say how I feel.
I can wish someone well.

C How healthy are you?

1 Vocabulary Healthy habits

A 🔊 Complete the phrases with the correct verbs. Then listen and check your answers.

eat	eat	exercise	get	go	lift	protect	wash

1. _____
   a balanced diet

2. _____
   your hands

3. _____
   your skin

4. _____
   weights

5. _____
   for a walk

6. _____
   daily

7. _____
   enough sleep

8. _____
   a good breakfast

B **Pair work** Which of the healthy habits in Part A do you have? Tell your partner.

2 Conversation I don't have much energy.

A 🔊 Listen and practice.

Laura: What's wrong, Hal? Are you OK?
Hal: Oh, hi, Laura. I don't know. I just don't have much energy.
Laura: Hmm. Do you eat breakfast every day?
Hal: Sure. And I exercise. I lift weights at my gym.
Laura: And how often do you go there?
Hal: Three or four days a week.
Laura: That's not bad. How long do you spend there?
Hal: Oh, about an hour a day.
Laura: That's good. And how much sleep do you get?
Hal: Quite a bit, about ten hours a night.
Laura: Ten hours? That's why you don't have any energy. I think that's too much sleep!

B 🔊 Listen to the rest of the conversation. What else does Laura ask about?

3 Grammar 🔊 *How* questions

How often do you go to the gym? Three or four days a week. **How long** do you spend at the gym? About an hour. **How well** do you follow your diet? Not very well.	**How healthy** are your eating habits? Somewhat healthy. **How many** meals do you eat a day? Five small meals. **How much** sleep do you get? Quite a bit.

A Complete the questions with a *How* question. Then compare with a partner.

1. _____ do you protect your skin from the sun?
   a. Extremely well.   b. Pretty well.   c. Not very well.

2. _____ are your eating habits?
   a. Very healthy.   b. Quite healthy.   c. Not healthy at all.

3. _____ coffee do you drink in a week?
   a. A lot.   b. Quite a bit.   c. Not much.

4. _____ do you eat red meat?
   a. Every day.   b. Several times a week.   c. Never.

5. _____ do you spend on the computer every week?
   a. 40 hours.   b. 20 hours.   c. Five hours.

6. _____ times a day do you wash your hands?
   a. About six times.   b. About three times.   c. Once.

B Pair work Ask and answer the questions in Part A. Circle your partner's answers.

A: *How well do you protect your skin from the sun?*
B: *Not very well. I sometimes wear a hat, but I rarely use sunscreen.*

4 Speaking Good question!

A Group work Look at the pictures. How many different *How* questions can you make for each picture? Ask the questions.

A: *How many times a week do you lift weights?*
B: *Never. I go to the gym once a week, but I don't lift weights.*
C: *How long do you spend at the gym?*

B How healthy do you think you are?

5 Keep talking!

Go to page 136 for more practice.

I can ask and talk about healthy habits. ☑

D Don't stress out!

1 Reading 🔊

A Read the article. Write the correct headings above the paragraphs.

| Communicate | Breathe | Do Nothing | Move! | Laugh | Get Organized |

FEELING STRESSED?

Everyone feels stress, and a little stress is OK. It's what gives you energy and pushes you to do well at school or work. But too much stress is not good. There are ways to manage stress. Try one or more of these tips the next time you feel stressed out.

1. _____

Take a deep breath. Breathe slowly and deeply every time you begin to feel stress. Make this a habit, and you can often stop a little stress from becoming a lot of stress.

2. _____

Make a "to do" list, and decide what you need to do right away and what can easily wait. Clean up your study or work space. Do the same with your computer desktop.

3. _____

Go for a swim. Run. Ride your bicycle. Do aerobics. Hike up a mountain. It doesn't really matter what you do. Just do something that you enjoy.

4. _____

Have a problem? Don't keep it inside. Talk to a friend, a family member, or even your cat. Don't want to talk? Write it down in a stress journal.

5. _____

See a funny movie. Tell some jokes. Watch some silly pet videos on the Internet. Laughter – yours or someone else's – is often the best medicine.

6. _____

That's right . . . nothing! Close the door. No TV, computer, or phone. Sit down and take a break from life. Close your eyes and feel the stress . . . disappear.

▶ ◀ 1:41 / 2:37 ━━━━━━━━━○━━━ ☑

B Read the article again. Write the tip number next to what each person does to manage stress.

_____ **Jill:** I watch my favorite TV show, and I laugh and laugh.

_____ **Rachid:** I go jogging. It makes me feel better.

_____ **Paul:** I just sit quietly. That's all I do!

_____ **Valerie:** I clean my house and put everything away.

_____ **Ming:** I stop and breathe deeply.

_____ **Eduardo:** I call a good friend and talk for a while.

C Pair work Which tips in Part A do you think work? Tell your partner.

2 Listening It works for me!

A 🔊 Listen to four people talk about how they manage stress. What do they do?
Number the pictures from 1 to 4. There are two extra items.

B 🔊 Listen again. What else do the people do to manage stress? Write the activities.

1. _____   3. _____
2. _____   4. _____

3 Writing Managing stress

A Think about how you manage stress. Answer the questions.

- How much stress do you feel?
- What makes you stressed?
- How well do you manage stress?
- What do you do?

B Write a paragraph about how you manage stress.
Use the model and your answers in Part A to
help you.

C Pair work Share your writing. Do the same
things stress you out?

> *How I Manage Stress*
> *I don't often feel stressed, but*
> *Mondays are sometimes difficult.*
> *I'm a full-time student, but I have a*
> *part-time job on Mondays. Here are*
> *a few ways I manage stress on*
> *Mondays. I eat a good breakfast and*
> *lift weights. Then I go to school early*
> *and talk with friends. It really helps.*

4 Speaking Living with stress

Pair work Imagine you are one of these people. Ask your partner for tips to help
you manage your stress.

- A mother with two young children and no time
- A young man before his wedding
- A soccer player before a big game
- A student before a big test

A: *I'm very tired, and my children never stop. What can I do?*
B: *Talk to your friends and find out what they do.*

I can discuss ways to manage stress. ☑

Wrap-up

1 Quick pair review

Lesson A **Test your partner!** Say the name of a sport. Can your partner say what parts of the body you use for the sport? Take turns. You have one minute.

A: *Soccer.*
B: *Legs, feet, head . . .*

Lesson B **Brainstorm!** Make a list of ways to say how you feel and ways to wish someone well. You have two minutes.

Lesson C **Do you remember?** Complete the questions with *much, well, healthy, many,* and *long*. You have one minute.

1. How _____ apples do you eat a week?
2. How _____ stress do you have at work?
3. How _____ do you work on Saturdays?
4. How _____ is your lifestyle?
5. How _____ do you manage stress?

Lesson D **Guess!** Act out a way to manage stress. Can your partner guess what it is? Take turns. You have one minute.

A: *Are you exercising?*
B: *Yes, I am.*

2 In the real world

What other ways can you manage stress? Go online and find three ideas in English. Then write about them.

> *Three Ways to Manage Stress*
> *Turn off your computer and your phone for an hour. Then turn on some relaxing music. Open a good book. . . .*

What's on TV?

LESSON **A**	LESSON **B**	LESSON **C**	LESSON **D**
• Types of TV shows • Verb + infinitive or gerund	• Agreeing with an opinion • Disagreeing with an opinion	• Television • Present continuous for future plans	• Reading: "Reality Shows" • Writing: My favorite TV show

Warm-up

1. ☐

2. ☐

3. ☐

4. ☐

5. ☐

6. ☐

A Match the popular TV shows with the years they started. Check your answers on page 64.

   a. 1958   b. 1960   c. 1976   d. 1981   e. 1994   f. 2002

B Can you name a show for each decade from your country? Do you watch the shows now?

A *I love watching game shows.*

1 Vocabulary Types of TV shows

A 🔊 Match the TV shows and the pictures. Then listen and check your answers.

a. a cartoon	d. a game show	g. a sitcom
b. a documentary	e. the news	h. a soap opera
c. a drama	f. a reality show	i. a talk show

1. [c]

2. [g]

3. [ ]

4. [ ]

5. [ ]

6. [ ]

7. [ ]

8. [ ]

9. [ ]

B Pair work What was the last show you watched on TV? What type of show was it? Tell your partner.

"I watched a cartoon with my son. It was . . ."

2 Language in context TV preferences

A 🔊 Listen to four people talk about their TV preferences. Who doesn't watch TV very much?

I watch a lot of TV. I really enjoy baseball. And I hope to get a big new TV soon.

– *Jessica*

I love soap operas. My favorite is *Our Life*. I like seeing my favorite actors.

– *Lucas*

I don't like reality shows at all. I love to watch documentaries and game shows.

– *Gustavo*

I hardly ever watch TV. I prefer to listen to the radio. I hate to miss the news.

– *Min-hwa*

B Which person in Part A are you similar to?

3 Grammar 🔊 Verb + infinitive or gerund

Verb + infinitive	**Verb + infinitive or gerund**
I **hope to get** a big TV.	I **like to see / seeing** my favorite actors.
I **want to see** every baseball game.	I **love to watch / watching** game shows.
	I **prefer to listen / listening** to the radio.
Verb + gerund	I **hate to miss / missing** the news.
I **enjoy watching** football games.	
I **dislike watching** TV.	

A Circle the correct verb forms. If both forms are correct, circle both.
Then practice with a partner.

1. **A:** What types of TV shows do you like **to watch / watching** late at night?

   B: Actually, I dislike **to watch / watching** TV at night. I prefer **to be / being** online.

2. **A:** What do you want **to watch / watching** on TV tonight? A reality show?

   B: I hate **to watch / watching** those shows. I enjoy **to watch / watching** dramas.

3. **A:** Do you want **to see / seeing** a movie tonight?

   B: No, not tonight. My favorite TV show is on, and I hate **to miss / missing** it.

B Complete the questions with a correct form of the verb. Then compare with
a partner.

1. Do you enjoy _____ (watch) cartoons on TV?

2. What do you want _____ (watch) on TV this weekend?

3. Do you like _____ (guess) the answers on game shows?

4. What types of TV shows do you dislike _____ (watch)?

C Pair work Ask and answer the questions in Part B. Answer with your
own information.

4 Speaking TV talk

A Add one more thing to the chart.

Find someone who . . .	Name
1. enjoys watching documentaries	
2. wants to buy a new TV	
3. hopes to meet a famous actress or actor	
4. hates missing soap operas	
5.	

B Class activity Find classmates for each sentence. Write their names.

   A: *Do you enjoy watching documentaries?*
   B: *Yes, I do.*

5 Keep talking!

Go to page 137 for more practice.

I *can* talk about types of TV shows I like. ☑

57

1 Interactions · Agreeing and disagreeing

A Look at the picture. What are the people doing? Do you think they like the TV show?

B 🔊 Listen to the conversation. Why doesn't Vasco like talk shows?
Then practice the conversation.

Fred: Let's see what's on TV. . . . Oh, no! I don't like this talk show at all. I think it's terrible.

Vasco: I agree. Actually, I hate all talk shows. I think they're really boring.

Fred: Really? I disagree. I think some of them are pretty interesting.

Vasco: I don't think any talk shows are interesting.

Fred: Well, would you like to watch something else?

C 🔊 Listen to the expressions. Then practice the conversation again with the new expressions.

Agreeing with an opinion	*Disagreeing with an opinion*
I agree. I agree with you. I think so, too.	I disagree. I don't really agree. I'm afraid I disagree.

D Complete each response with one of the expressions from Part C. Then practice with a partner.

1. **A:** Most TV sitcoms are funny.   **B:** _____ I never laugh at them.
2. **A:** Reality shows are great.   **B:** _____ I watch them all the time.
3. **A:** Game shows are exciting.   **B:** _____ I think they're boring.
4. **A:** It's good to watch the news.   **B:** _____ I watch it every night.
5. **A:** Cartoons are just for children.   **B:** _____ They're for adults, too.

2 Listening What else is on?

A 🔊 Listen to Dan and Amy discuss what is on TV. Number the TV shows from 1 to 5. (There is one extra picture.)

B 🔊 Listen again. Look at Amy's opinion of each show. Write Dan's opinion.

Amy's opinions: Dan's opinions:

1. boring   1. _____
2. great   2. _____
3. interesting   3. _____
4. exciting   4. _____
5. fantastic   5. _____

3 Speaking My opinion

A Check (✓) the statements you agree with. Then make the statements you disagree with true for you.

                    exciting

☐ Documentaries are ~~boring~~.

☐ Talk shows are very interesting.

☐ All sports programs are exciting.

☐ Most sitcoms are very funny.

☐ It's important to watch the TV news.

☐ Reality shows are boring.

B **Group work** Share your ideas.

> **A:** *In my opinion, documentaries are exciting.*
> **B:** *I don't really agree. I think they're pretty boring.*
> **C:** *What about talk shows? I think they're very interesting.*
> **A:** *I agree with you.*

I can agree and disagree with an opinion.

C I'm recording a documentary.

1 Vocabulary Television

A 🔊 Match the words and the definitions. Then listen and check your answers.

1. I often **record** my favorite show. __c__
2. I usually **fast-forward** through the boring parts of shows. _____
3. I always **skip** the sad parts of movies. _____
4. I watch **reruns** of old sitcoms. _____
5. I never lose the **remote control.** _____
6. Most **commercials** are funny. _____
7. You can learn a lot from **public TV.** _____
8. I think **satellite TV** is great. _____

a. to play a show at high speed
b. to not watch something
c. to store a show to watch it later
d. advertisements for products
e. a nonprofit TV network
f. a service that sends TV shows to homes through a dish
g. repeat showings of a TV show
h. a device used to control a TV from a distance

B Pair work Which sentences in Part A describe your opinions or habits? Tell your partner.

A: *I often record my favorite show.*
B: *Really? I never record my favorite show.*

2 Conversation I'm going away this weekend.

A 🔊 Listen and practice.

Nora: Hi, Zack. How are you?
Zack: Oh, hi, Nora. I'm fine. Actually, I'm going away this weekend, so I want to record some TV shows.
Nora: Really? Which shows?
Zack: On Friday night, I'm recording the soccer game. The Hawks are playing the Lions.
Nora: Oh, I'm watching that at Lisa's. She's having a soccer party. She has satellite TV now.
Zack: Well, I'm watching it on Sunday night. That way I can fast-forward and skip the commercials.
Nora: Good idea. I hate watching commercials. So what else are you recording?
Zack: On Saturday, I'm recording a documentary on Channel 11 called *TV Is Dead.*

B 🔊 Listen to the rest of the conversation. What is Nora watching on TV this weekend?

60

3 Grammar 🔊 | **Present continuous for future plans**

I'm **recording** the soccer game.	**Is** Zack **watching** the game on Sunday?
I'm **not recording** the sitcom.	Yes, he **is**. No, he**'s not**. / No, he **isn't**.
She**'s having** a soccer party this week.	**Are** they **watching** the game on Sunday?
She**'s not visiting** her family.	Yes, they **are**. No, they**'re not**. / No, they **aren't**.
They**'re playing** the Lions this weekend.	What else **are** you **recording** on Friday?
They**'re not playing** the Sharks.	I'm also recording a movie.

A Complete these conversations with the present continuous form of the verbs. Then practice with a partner.

1. **A:** What _____ you _____ (do) this weekend? _____ you _____ (go) anywhere?

   B: No, I _____ (stay) home all weekend. Some friends _____ (come) over to watch a basketball game. The Tigers _____ (play).

2. **A:** I _____ (get) satellite TV on Wednesday – finally! What _____ you _____ (do) on Friday? Do you want to come over?

   B: I'd love to, but I can't. Joe and I _____ (visit) his parents this weekend. We _____ (leave) on Friday after work.

B What are you doing this weekend? Use these verbs to write about your weekend plans. Then tell your partner.

1. (meet) _____   3. (play) _____
2. (watch) _____   4. (go out) _____

4 Pronunciation Sentence stress

🔊 Listen and repeat. Notice how the important words in a sentence are stressed.

I'm **going** to **Colombia** on **Monday**.   She's **staying home** this **weekend**.

5 Speaking What are you recording?

A Imagine you're going away next week, and you can't watch TV. Decide where you're going and make a list of five shows you are recording.

B **Class activity** Compare lists. Is anyone recording the same shows? Find classmates with a similar list.

A: *I'm visiting my mother next Tuesday, so I'm recording . . .*
B: *Me, too. I love . . . , and I'm recording . . .*

6 Keep talking!

Go to page **138** for more practice.

Go to page **138** for more practice.

I can describe future plans. ☑

D Popular TV

1 Reading 🔊

A Read the article. Match the headings and the descriptions of the reality shows.

a. Improvement shows   b. Game-style shows   c. Documentary-style shows

Reality Shows – you either love them or you hate them! But did you realize there are different types of reality shows? Read on and find out more. . . .

☐ In this type of reality show, **contestants** try to win a prize. The prize is often money or, in some cases, a job. Each week, one person leaves the show until there is only one – the winner. Sometimes the contestants vote on who stays or goes, sometimes the TV **viewers** at home vote, and other times the show's **judges** choose. One example is *Top Chef*. In this show, contestants cook dishes for the **host** and the three judges. The winner usually receives money, a trip, and an article in a food magazine.

☐ This type of reality show looks like a soap opera, but it is about one or more real people and their daily lives. Some of these shows are about people on the job, such as police officers, firefighters, or hospital workers. Others are about regular people in unusual situations, and some even follow famous people. One example of this type was *The Osbournes*. This show was about the daily life of British singer Ozzy Osbourne and his family. In these types of shows, there is no prize money and no winner.

☐ These shows are about a person or people who need a change. Other people help this person in one area, such as home, style, health, or relationships. An example of this is *What Not to Wear*. On this show, two hosts give fashion advice to someone who needs a new "look." The hosts go to the person's closet and throw away clothes that they don't like. The person then receives money and a trip to New York City to shop for new clothes.

B Read the article again. Look at the questions. Check (✓) the correct answers.

Which show . . . ?	*Top Chef*	*The Osbournes*	*What Not to Wear*
gives money			
gives a trip			
has celebrities			
is about fashion			
is like a soap opera			

C Find the words in **bold** in the article. What do they mean? Match the definitions and the correct word.

A person / People who . . .

a. presents a TV show _____

b. participate in a competition _____

c. watch a television program _____

d. decide who wins or loses _____

D Pair work Imagine you can be on one type of reality show. Which would you choose? Why? Tell your partner.

2 Listening Favorite shows back home

A 🔊 Listen to three students talk about their favorite TV shows in their countries. What type of show does each like? Write it in the chart.

	Type of show	Favorite thing about the show	
Valerie		the models	the end of each show
Young-ho		the costumes	the actors
Claudia		the teenagers	the stories

B 🔊 Listen again. What is their favorite thing about the show? Circle the correct answers.

3 Writing My favorite TV show

A Think of your favorite TV show. Answer the questions.

- What type of show is it?
- What happens on the show?
- Why do you enjoy watching it?
- Is there anything you don't like about it?

B Write a paragraph about your favorite TV show. Use the model and your answers in Part A to help you.

C Group work Share your writing. Do you agree with each other's opinions?

> *My Favorite TV Show*
> *I like to watch the reality show "Project Runway." The contestants are fashion students. The winner receives money and an article in a fashion magazine. I enjoy watching the show because the clothes are fantastic, but sometimes I disagree with the judges.*

4 Speaking Reality shows

A Group work Read about these reality shows. Which ones sound interesting? Why?

The Amazing Race
the U.S.
Pairs race one another around the world. The winners receive a million dollars.

StarStruck
the Philippines
Teens compete in a talent show. It's famous for the saying "Dream. Believe. Survive."

How Clean Is Your House?
the U.K.
Two cleaners visit homes and clean them up. They share their top cleaning tips.

B Do you ever watch similar shows in your country? Why or why not?

"I watch a show similar to StarStruck. I don't really like it, but I always watch it!"

> *I can give my opinions about popular TV shows.* ☑

Wrap-up

1 Quick pair review

Lesson A **Brainstorm!** Make a list of types of TV shows. How many do you remember? You have one minute.

Lesson B **Do you remember?** Write A for expressions that show you agree with an opinion. Write D for expressions that show you disagree. You have one minute.

1. I disagree. _____
2. I think so, too. _____
3. I agree. _____
4. I don't really agree. _____
5. I'm afraid I disagree. _____
6. I agree with you. _____

Lesson C **Find out!** What are three things both you and your partner are doing next week? Take turns. You and your partner have two minutes.

A: *I'm watching a baseball game next week. Are you?*
B: *Yes, I am.*

Lesson D **Guess!** Describe your favorite TV show, but don't say its name. Can your partner guess the name and the type of show it is? Take turns. You and your partner have two minutes.

A: *In this TV show, celebrities dance with professional dancers.*
B: *Is it a reality show?*
A: *Yes, it is.*
B: *Is it Dancing with the Stars?*
A: *Yes, it is.*

2 In the real world

What new shows are on TV this year? Look at a TV schedule or go online and find information about a new TV show in English. Then write about it.

- What's the name of the TV show?
- What type of TV show is it?
- What's it about?
- When is it on?

> *A New TV Show*
> *"Three Rivers" is a drama. It's about*
> *a hospital. . . .*

Favorites

Group work Play the game. Put a small object on *Start*. Toss a coin.

 Move 1 space.   Move 2 spaces.

Heads   Tails

Use the correct form of *be* to ask and answer questions. Can you answer the questions? Take turns.

Yes. → Move ahead.   No. ← Move back.

A: *Are you interested in travel?*
B: *Yes, I am. I'm interested in new places.*

1 **START**

2 _____ you interested in travel?

3 Who _____ your favorite singer?

4 _____ your friends interested in politics?

5 What _____ your favorite day of the week?

Su	M	T	W	Th	F	Sa
			1	2	3	4	5
6	7	8	9	10	11	12
13	14	15	16	17	18	19

6 What _____ your favorite food?

7 What _____ your favorite drink?

8 Who _____ your favorite artist?

9 What _____ your favorite song?

10 _____ you interested in fashion?

11 What _____ your favorite book?

12 _____ your teacher interested in sports?

13 What _____ your favorite animal?

14 _____ your grandparents interested in technology?

15 What _____ your favorite place for vacation?

16 **FINISH**

An active class?

A Add two things to the chart.

Find someone who . . .	Name	Extra information
goes to a gym		
plays table tennis		
does gymnastics		
plays soccer on weekends		
plays a sport with a family member		
exercises in the morning		
watches baseball on TV		
listens to sports on the radio		
dislikes sports		

B Class activity Find classmates who do each thing. Ask more questions. Write their name and extra information you hear.

A: *Do you go to a gym, Anna?*
B: *Yes, I do. I go three times a week.*
A: *Really? What do you do there?*
B: *I do yoga, and I swim.*

Help box

How often do you . . . ?
Where do you . . . ?
Who do you . . . with?
What's your favorite . . . ?

C Pair work Share your information.

A: *Anna goes to the gym three times a week.*
B: *Really? What does she do there?*

Are you confident?

A **Pair work** Take the quiz. Take turns asking and answering the questions.

1. What colors do you often wear?
   a. I wear red, pink, and orange.
   b. I wear yellow and green.
   c. I wear blue and purple.
   d. I wear black, white, and gray.

2. What are you like around friends?
   a. I'm always very talkative.
   b. I'm talkative, but sometimes I'm quiet.
   c. I'm usually the quiet one.
   d. I don't know.

3. How do you enter a party?
   a. I walk in and say hello to everyone.
   b. I walk in and say hello to one person.
   c. I walk in and look for a friend.
   d. I walk in and stand in a corner.

4. You meet someone new. What do you do?
   a. I say hello and ask questions.
   b. I say "hi" and wait for questions.
   c. I just smile.
   d. I look away.

5. You see someone you like. What do you do?
   a. I walk up and say hello.
   b. I ask a friend to introduce us.
   c. I smile at the person.
   d. I do nothing.

6. The teacher asks a question. What do you do?
   a. I shout out the answer.
   b. I raise my hand.
   c. I check my answer with a friend.
   d. I look down at my desk.

B **Pair work** Add up and score your quizzes. Are the results true for you?

A: *I got 17 points.*
B: *You're very confident!*
A: *Really? I'm not sure about that.*

| a answers = 3 points | c answers = 1 point |
| b answers = 2 points | d answers = 0 points |

12–18 You're very confident. Aren't you ever shy?
6–11 You're confident, but not about everything.
0–5 You're not very confident. Believe in yourself!

Find the differences

Student A

Pair work You and your partner have pictures of the same people, but six things are different. Describe the pictures and ask questions to find the differences. Circle them.

A: *In my picture, Brian is young. Is he young in your picture?*
B: *Yeah, so that's the same. In my picture, he has short straight hair.*
A: *Mine, too. What color is . . . ?*

What's the weather like?

Student A

A Pair work You and your partner have information about the weather in four cities, but some information is missing. Ask questions to get the information.

> A: *When is spring in Lisbon?*
> B: *It's from March to June. What's the weather like in the spring?*
> A: *It's warm and sunny.*

Lisbon, Portugal

Season	Months	Weather
Spring	March–June	warm and sunny
Summer	June–September	
Fall	September–December	
Winter	December–March	cool and rainy

Seoul, South Korea

Season	Months	Weather
Spring	March–June	
Summer	June–September	hot and rainy
Fall	September–December	
Winter	December–March	very cold, snowy

Sydney, Australia

Season	Months	Weather
Spring	September–December	warm and sunny
Summer	December–March	
Fall	March–June	
Winter	June–September	cool and windy

Buenos Aires, Argentina

Season	Months	Weather
Spring	September–December	
Summer	December–March	sometimes hot, not rainy
Fall	March–June	
Winter	June–September	cold, not rainy

B Pair work Which city's seasons are similar to yours?

Find the differences

Student B

Pair work You and your partner have pictures of the same people, but six things are different. Describe the pictures and ask questions to find the differences. Circle them.

A: *In my picture, Brian is young. Is he young in your picture?*
B: *Yeah, so that's the same. In my picture, he has short straight hair.*
A: *Mine, too. What color is . . . ?*

What's the weather like?

Student B

A Pair work You and your partner have information about the weather in four cities, but some information is missing. Ask questions to get the information.

A: *When is spring in Lisbon?*
B: *It's from March to June. What's the weather like in the spring?*
A: *It's warm and sunny.*

Lisbon, Portugal	Season	Months	Weather
	Spring	March–June	
	Summer	June–September	hot, not rainy
	Fall	September–December	warm and windy
	Winter	December–March	

Seoul, South Korea	Season	Months	Weather
	Spring	March–June	warm, not rainy
	Summer	June–September	
	Fall	September–December	sunny and cool
	Winter	December–March	

Sydney, Australia	Season	Months	Weather
	Spring	September–December	
	Summer	December–March	hot and dry
	Fall	March–June	cool and rainy
	Winter	June–September	

Buenos Aires, Argentina	Season	Months	Weather
	Spring	September–December	warm and rainy
	Summer	December–March	
	Fall	March–June	rainy, not cool
	Winter	June–September	

B Pair work Which city's seasons are similar to yours?

Someday . . .

A Write information about things you'd like to do someday.

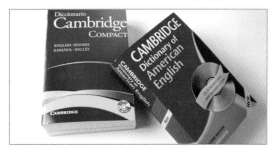

a language I'd like to learn: _____

a person I'd like to meet: _____

a country I'd like to visit: _____

a job I'd like to have: _____

something I'd like to buy: _____

a sport I'd like to try: _____

a place I'd like to live: _____

a game I'd like to play: _____

B **Group work** Share your ideas. Ask and answer questions for more information.

A: *I think I'd like to learn Spanish someday.*
B: *Really? Why?*
A: *Because I'd like to visit Costa Rica.*

Home sweet home

A **Pair work** Look at the picture for two minutes. Try to remember the rooms, furniture, and other details.

B **Pair work** Cover the picture. Ask and answer these questions. What do you remember?

- How many rooms are there in the house?
- Which rooms are on the first floor? the second floor?
- How much light is there in the living room? How many windows are there?
- Is there much furniture in the living room? What's there?
- What's on the coffee table? What's on the kitchen table?
- Are there many pictures in the house? Where are they?
- How are the two bedrooms different?
- How are the two bathrooms different?
- Is there much space in this house? Do you think there's much noise?

   A: *How many rooms are there in the house?*
   B: *I think there are . . . rooms.*
   A: *I think so, too. Which rooms are on the first floor?*

C Look at the picture again, and check your answers.

Cleanup time

Pair work You need to do some chores around the apartment. Decide who does each chore. Be fair!

A: *Could you take out the garbage?*
B: *Sure. I can take it out. Would you clean out the closet?*

Don't get up!

Student A

A **Pair work** Tell your partner to cover the pictures. Describe the exercises. Your partner does the actions. Take turns.

Eye exercises

Move your eyes quickly to the right. Then move them quickly to the left. Repeat five times.

Wrist exercises

Stretch your arms in front of you. Move your hands up and down quickly. Repeat five times.

Shoulder exercises

Lift your shoulders slowly to your ears. Don't move, and hold for three seconds. Then lower your shoulders. Repeat three times.

> **A:** *Move your eyes to the right.*
> **B:** *Like this?*
> **A:** *Yes. Now move them to the left.*

B How did your partner do? How does your partner feel?

Student B

A **Pair work** Tell your partner to cover the pictures. Describe the exercises. Your partner does the actions. Take turns.

Hand exercises

Stretch your arms in front of you. Close your hands. Then open your hands quickly. Repeat five times.

Neck exercises

Touch your right ear to your right shoulder. Then touch your left ear to your left shoulder. Repeat five times.

Arm exercises

Lift your right arm up and down. Then lift your left arm up and down. Repeat three times.

> **B:** *Stretch your arms in front of you.*
> **A:** *Like this?*
> **B:** *Yes. Now close your hands.*

B How did your partner do? How does your partner feel?

How healthy are you?

A Pair work Take the quiz. Take turns asking and answering the questions.

1. How many servings of fruit and vegetables do you eat a day?
   - a. Five or more
   - b. Three to four
   - c. One to two

2. How often do you eat breakfast?
   - a. Every day
   - b. Two to six times a week
   - c. Rarely

3. How many meals do you eat a day?
   - a. Four or five small meals
   - b. Three meals
   - c. One or two big meals

4. How much junk food do you eat?
   - a. Very little
   - b. About average
   - c. A lot

5. How often do you exercise?
   - a. Every day
   - b. Two or three times a week
   - c. Never

6. How long do you spend watching TV or playing video games each week?
   - a. One to two hours
   - b. Three to six hours
   - c. Seven or more hours

7. How well do you sleep at night?
   - a. Very well
   - b. Pretty well
   - c. Not very well

8. How often do you get a checkup?
   - a. Once a year
   - b. Every two or three years
   - c. Hardly ever

9. How happy are you with your health?
   - a. Very happy
   - b. Pretty happy
   - c. Not very happy

a answers = 3 points
b answers = 2 points
c answers = 1 point

21–27 You're very healthy. Congratulations!
15–20 You're pretty healthy. Keep it up!
9–14 You can improve your health. Start now!

B Pair work Add up and score your quizzes. Are the results true for you? Why or why not?

A: *My score is 16. It says I'm pretty healthy. I think that's true.*
B: *My score is 20, but I think I'm very healthy.*

TV listings

A **Pair work** Look at the TV listings. What types of shows are they?

	Channel 4	Channel 11	Channel 13
7:00–7:30	**Win or Lose** Everyone's favorite game show! Play at home!	**Soap Stars on Ice** See your favorite soap stars ice skate for charity!	**Man's Best Friend** A new sitcom about a talking horse named Fred
7:30–8:00	**Under Arrest** Police drama starring Damien Porter		**Travels with Ryan** This week, Ryan learns to samba in Brazil.
8:00–8:30	**Mr. and Mrs. Right** The best reality show on TV! Vote for your favorite couple!	**The Year in Sports** The best baseball moments of the year	**The Ina Lopez Show** Tough questions, honest answers. Tonight talk-show queen Ina takes your calls!
8:30–9:00		**Meet My Family** A funny family sitcom	
9:00–9:30	**Lions of Kenya** "An amazing documentary"	**Take It or Leave It** Part game show, part reality show. New!	**My Roommate Ralph** A new sitcom from the creators of *Alien Mom*
9:30–10:00	**The News** Local news with Dinah and Jim	**Family Life** The funny new cartoon for adults	**Kiss and Tell** See the soap everyone is talking about!

B **Pair work** Look at the information about the Green family. They have only one TV. What shows can they watch together from 7:00 to 10:00?

Dan Green	**Sarah Green**	**Rick Green**	**Rose Green**
• enjoys watching sports and news	• hopes to visit Rio de Janeiro	• loves to watch game shows	• enjoys watching soap operas
• hates to watch reality shows	• prefers to watch funny shows	• hates soap operas	• doesn't like watching sitcoms

A: *They can watch* Win or Lose *at 7:00. Rick loves to watch game shows.*
B: *And they can watch* Travels with Ryan *at 7:30. Sarah hopes to visit Brazil.*

C **Group work** What shows do you want to watch?

My daily planner

A Make a schedule for tomorrow afternoon and evening. Use the ideas below and your own ideas. Write four activities in the daily planner. Think about how long each activity will take.

go grocery shopping   meet friends for coffee   watch a movie on TV

watch sports with friends   chat online with friends   clean my room

exercise at the gym   watch the news   study at the library

_____   _____   _____

Date   /   /   Sun Mon Tues Wed Thurs Fri Sat   Notes
2:00
2:30
3:00
3:30
4:00
4:30
5:00
5:30

Date   /   /   Sun Mon Tues Wed Thurs Fri Sat   Notes
6:00
6:30
7:00
7:30
8:00
8:30
9:00
9:30

B Class activity Think of three fun activities. Find classmates who want to do the activities with you. Add the information to your planners.

A: *What are you doing tomorrow evening at 7:00?*
B: *I'm meeting some friends for coffee.*
A: *Oh, OK. Do you want to see a movie at 8:00?*
B: *I'd love to, but I can't. I'm . . .*

Irregular verbs

Base form	Simple past	Past participle
be	was, were	been
become	became	become
build	built	built
buy	bought	bought
choose	chose	chosen
come	came	come
do	did	done
draw	drew	drawn
drink	drank	drunk
drive	drove	driven
eat	ate	eaten
feel	felt	felt
get	got	gotten
give	gave	given
go	went	gone
hang	hung	hung
have	had	had
hear	heard	heard
hold	held	held
know	knew	known
leave	left	left
lose	lost	lost
make	made	made

Base form	Simple past	Past participle
meet	met	met
pay	paid	paid
put	put	put
read	read	read
ride	rode	ridden
run	ran	run
say	said	said
see	saw	seen
sell	sold	sold
send	sent	sent
sing	sang	sung
sit	sat	sat
sleep	slept	slept
speak	spoke	spoken
spend	spent	spent
stand	stood	stood
swim	swam	swum
take	took	taken
teach	taught	taught
think	thought	thought
wear	wore	worn
win	won	won
write	wrote	written

Credits

Illustration credits

Photography credits

Four Corners

Jack C. Richards · David Bohlke

2A

Video Activity Sheets

CAMBRIDGE
UNIVERSITY PRESS

1 *Unusual interests*

Before you watch

A Look at the picture. Answer the questions. Then compare with a partner.

Emi

1. Where is Emi?

_____

2. What is Emi's job?

_____

3. What is Emi doing?

_____

B Match the words and the pictures. Then compare with a partner.

| a. collect buttons | b. make a sweater | c. make jewelry | d. play chess |

1. ☐

2. ☐

3. ☐

4. ☐

While you watch

A Who does each thing? Check (✓) the correct answers. (More than one answer is possible.)

	Emi	Tim	Alicia	The man in the park
1. Who collects buttons?	☐	☐	☐	☐
2. Who plays chess?	☐	☐	☐	☐
3. Who makes jewelry?	☐	☐	☐	☐
4. Who makes sweaters?	☐	☐	☐	☐

B Read the sentences about Tim's collection. Write T (true) or F (false).

1. Tim has about a thousand buttons. _____

2. He buys them on vacation. _____

3. Friends and family members also give the buttons to him. _____

4. Emi doesn't like the button from Tim's sister. _____

5. His sister lives in Brazil now. _____

6. Tim gives Emi a button. _____

C Read the sentences about Alicia's interest. Circle the correct answers.

1. Alicia makes jewelry because it's _____.

   a. hard   b. fun   c. boring

2. The necklace takes a few _____ to make.

   a. minutes   b. hours   c. days

3. _____ are a little difficult to make.

   a. Necklaces   b. Earrings   c. Necklaces and earrings

4. Alicia doesn't _____ her jewelry.

   a. buy   b. make   c. sell

5. Alicia makes jewelry as a _____.

   a. job   b. hobby   c. homework assignment

After you watch

A Pair work What do you think about Emi, Tim, and Alicia's interests?
Do you know anyone with the same interests as them? Tell your partner.

   A: I think Tim's hobby is interesting.

   B: Me, too. Do you collect buttons from different places?

   A: No, I don't. But I collect postcards.

B Group work Interview four classmates about their interests. Complete the chart with their information.

Name	Interest or hobby	Why he or she likes it
Roberto	does karate	It's good exercise.

C Group work Tell another group about your classmates' interests and hobbies.

"Roberto does karate. He likes karate because it's good exercise."

Happy birthday, Eric!

Before you watch

A Complete the sentences with the correct names. Then compare with a partner.

1. _____ has short curly brown hair.

2. _____ has long straight blond hair.

3. _____ has short straight brown hair.

4. _____ has short gray hair.

5. _____ and _____ are middle-aged.

6. _____ is elderly.

7. _____ is young.

B What do your family and friends usually do on your birthday? Check (✓) the items.

☐ eat out with me   ☐ make a video for me
☐ give me a gift   ☐ make special food for me
☐ go dancing with me   ☐ sing "Happy Birthday!" to me
☐ have a party for me   ☐ other: _____

C Group work Share your information from Part B. Ask and answer questions for more information.

A: My mother usually makes me a special meal on my birthday.

B: That's nice! What does she make?

While you watch

A Circle the correct answers.

1. Right now, Eric is _____.

   a. at home   b. in California   c. in Italy

2. He is _____ there.

   a. at school   b. on vacation   c. working

3. Today is Eric's _____ birthday.

   a. 18th   b. 20th   c. 22nd

4. Eric's Aunt Lily has the _____.

   a. birthday cake   b. gift   c. video camera

5. Eric's family _____.

   a. eats the cake   b. shows Eric pictures   c. sings "Happy Birthday"

B Write T (true) or F (false).

1. Now Eric has blond hair. _____

2. Eric plays the guitar. _____

3. Eric draws pictures. _____

4. His sister Lizzy plays the piano. _____

5. Eric's family took a trip to Florida. _____

C Who describes Eric with the words below? Check (✓) the correct answers.
(More than one answer is possible.)

	Mom	Dad	Lizzy	Grandpa Joe
1. creative	☐	☐	☐	☐
2. funny	☐	☐	☐	☐
3. handsome	☐	☐	☐	☐
4. hardworking	☐	☐	☐	☐
5. serious	☐	☐	☐	☐
6. short	☐	☐	☐	☐
7. tall	☐	☐	☐	☐

After you watch

A Pair work Do you like Eric's birthday video? Do you want a birthday video from your family? Why or why not? Tell your partner.

B Pair work Interview your partner about a friend or family member. Complete the chart with his or her answers.

Questions	Name: _____
1. Is this person a friend or family member?	
2. What is his or her name?	
3. What is he or she like?	
4. What does he or she look like?	

C Group work Tell another pair about your partner's friend or family member.

"Sandra's sister is friendly and talkative. She's tall and thin, and has long, wavy hair."

January or July?

Before you watch

A Look at the pictures of Vancouver, Canada. Number the pictures from 1 to 3. Then compare with partner.

1. Vancouver is a great place to ski in the winter.

2. You can ride your bike in Vancouver in the spring or summer when it's warm.

3. You can see many colorful leaves in the park in the fall.

B Pair work Would you like to go on vacation in Vancouver? What would you like to do there? Tell your partner.

While you watch

A Circle the correct answers.

1. Ben has a _____.

   a. website   b. live travel blog   c. TV show

2. Ben and Nick want to get _____.

   a. emails and letters   b. phone calls and texts   c. emails and texts

3. The date is Thursday, _____ 14.

   a. January   b. May   c. July

4. Ben and Nick would like to talk about _____ Vancouver.

   a. the people in   b. the food in   c. a good time to visit

5. Ben and Nick have a problem because they want to _____ in Vancouver.

   a. do different things   b. eat different food   c. visit different friends

B Check (✓) the correct answers. (More than one answer is possible.)

	Ben	Ben's mom	Nick	Nick's mom
1. Who likes to ski?	☐	☐	☐	☐
2. Who wants to ride a bicycle?	☐	☐	☐	☐
3. Who doesn't like the snow?	☐	☐	☐	☐
4. Who thinks they should go in the spring?	☐	☐	☐	☐
5. Who thinks Ben and Nick's apartment isn't clean?	☐	☐	☐	☐

C Write T (true) or F (false).

1. Ben and Nick both want to go to Vancouver. _____

2. Ben wants to go in January. _____

3. Nick likes hot weather. _____

4. Nick and Ben's mothers are watching Ben's blog. _____

5. Ben and Nick agree on when to go to Vancouver. _____

After you watch

A Complete the summary with the correct words and expressions. Then compare with a partner. (There are two extra words.)

fall	park	problem	snows quite a bit	summer
opinion	pretty warm	ski	spring	winter

　　Ben and Nick have a _____. Ben wants to go to Vancouver in

the _____. He'd like to go to the _____.

　　But Nick wants to go in the _____ because he'd

like to _____. Nick's mom has a different

_____. She thinks spring is a good time because

it's _____ in the city, but it

_____ in the mountains.

B **Pair work** What's your opinion? When is a good time to visit Vancouver? Why?

"I'd say summer is a good time. I'd like to swim and walk in the park."

My new apartment!

Before you watch

A Match the pictures and the descriptions. Then compare with a partner.

1. ☐
_____

2. ☐
_____

3. ☐
_____

4. ☐
_____

5. ☐
_____

6. ☐
_____

a. There are a lot of dishes in the sink.
b. He is wiping off the counter.
c. There are a few magazines on the coffee table.
d. He is putting away his clothes.
e. There is a lot of light.
f. The room is a mess.

B Label the pictures in Part A with the correct names of the rooms. Then compare with a partner.

| bathroom | bedroom | kitchen | living room |

While you watch

A Write T (true) or F (false).

1. Tim and Bo's kitchen is a mess. _____

2. Bo usually puts the dishes away. _____

3. Tim watches TV and studies in the living room. _____

4. Tim and Bo's living room is clean. _____

5. Tim has a big bedroom, but there is a small closet. _____

B What's in Tim's apartment? Check (✓) the correct answers.

☐ a big closet	☐ a few boxes	☐ a lot of clothes	☐ a sofa
☐ books	☐ a few magazines	☐ a lot of garbage	☐ some noise
☐ a cat	☐ a guitar	☐ a lot of light	☐ a TV
☐ a dishwasher	☐ a lot of CDs	☐ a roommate	☐ two bedrooms

C Circle the correct answers.

1. Tim lives _____ his parents.

    a. near   b. far away from   c. next door to

2. Tim washes the dishes _____.

    a. every day   b. once a week   c. once a month

3. Bo is Tim's _____.

    a. student   b. classmate   c. roommate

4. Bo plays _____.

    a. the guitar   b. the piano   c. the drums

5. Tim says that Bo is a _____ guy.

    a. fun   b. creative   c. boring

6. Bo is a _____ person.

    a. clean   b. noisy   c. hardworking

After you watch

A What do you like about Tim's apartment? What don't you like? Make a list.

Things I like	Things I don't like
There is a big kitchen.	*The kitchen is a mess.*

B Pair work Make a request for each of the things you don't like in Part B. Your partner agrees to the requests. Take turns.

A: The kitchen is a mess. Could you clean it up, please?

B: No problem.

unit 5 *Don't stress out!*

Before you watch

A Match the stressful situations and the ways to manage them. Then compare with a partner.

1. Your computer broke, but you don't have enough money to buy a new one. _____

2. You have a big test tomorrow, but you don't know the information well. _____

3. You have a lot of work to do, but you don't have enough time to do it. _____

4. You want to exercise, but you don't have enough time. _____

a. Get help from other students in the class. Study with them.

b. Go to an Internet café or use a computer in a public library.

c. Walk to class more often and do quick exercises in the morning at home.

d. Ask someone to help you or decide which things you can do later.

B Pair work What do you do in each of the stressful situations in Part A? Tell your partner.

While you watch

A How does Marco manage his stress? Check (✓) the correct answers.

- ☐ He cleans up his apartment.
- ☐ He does aerobics.
- ☐ He does nothing.
- ☐ He does yoga.
- ☐ He listens to relaxing music.
- ☐ He meditates.
- ☐ He plays soccer.
- ☐ He plays video games.
- ☐ He reads a book.
- ☐ He talks to someone.
- ☐ He uses a stress ball.
- ☐ He watches a funny video.

B Marco explains how to meditate. Number the steps from 1 to 9.

_____ Close your eyes.

_____ Relax and watch your breath.

___1___ Sit comfortably.

_____ Breathe slowly and deeply.

_____ Cross your legs.

_____ Count the breaths silently.

_____ Put your hands on your knees.

_____ Keep your neck and back straight.

_____ Continue to breathe slowly and deeply.

C Write T (true) or F (false).

1. Marco is a student. _____

2. He has one part-time job. _____

3. He has a really hard class. _____

4. He has a big French test tomorrow. _____

5. Marco's number one tip is: Talk to somebody. _____

After you watch

A Pair work Which of Marco's tips for managing stress is your favorite? Why?

"My favorite tip is the stress ball. I use one of those, too."

B Group work Interview four classmates about their stress. Complete the chart with their answers.

Name	What makes you stressed?	How do you manage your stress?
Li-ming	*biology class; boss at work*	*swimming; TV; talk to friends*

C Class activity What is your number one tip for managing stress? Tell the class.

6 *Are you a star?*

Before you watch

Emi   Alicia   Ian

A Look at the pictures. Complete the sentences with the correct words.
Then compare with a partner.

| competition | contestants | judges | reality | star | win |

This is a _____ show. There are three _____.
They sing and dance on the show. Each one wants to be a _____.
Emi, Alicia, and Ian are the _____. They make comments
about the singers and the dancers. They help decide which one is going to
_____. Let the _____ begin!

B Pair work Can you make a new sentence with each of the words in Part A?
Tell your partner.

While you watch

A Write T (true) or F (false).

1. The contestants are shy and hardworking. _____

2. Some judges are friendly. _____

3. All of the contestants sing about TV shows. _____

4. Contestant 2 doesn't think Ian is nice. _____

5. Ian thinks Contestant 3 raps well. _____

B Who does each thing? Check (✓) the correct answers.

	Contestant 1	Contestant 2	Contestant 3
1. Who dances?	☐	☐	☐
2. Who writes songs?	☐	☐	☐
3. Who sings a song about love?	☐	☐	☐
4. Who sings a song about rainy day activities?	☐	☐	☐
5. Who sings a song about TV?	☐	☐	☐
6. Who does Ian tell to learn a new activity?	☐	☐	☐

C Which contestants are the judges talking about? Number the judges' comments 1, 2, or 3.

Judge	Comment	Contestant
Emi	I think you're really good!	
	You're hardworking and very noisy.	
	You're a really creative performer.	
Alicia	He's pretty cool!	
	You're funny and very exciting to watch!	
	That's a very interesting song.	
Ian	Do not sing again. Ever!	
	You dance like a refrigerator.	
	He's boring.	

After you watch

A Pair work Judge each contestant. Explain your opinions.

"Contestant number 3 is my favorite. He's a funny dancer. I didn't like . . ."

B Group work Discuss the questions.
- Do you enjoy watching TV talent shows? What is your opinion of them?
- Do you usually agree or disagree with the judges?
- Which singers are now famous for being on a TV talent show?

Credits

Photography credits

T-177 *(top)*, T-178, T-179, T-180, T-181, T-182, T-184, T-185, T-186, T-187
Video screen grabs courtesy of Steadman Productions, Boston, MA

Four Corners

Jack C. Richards · David Bohlke

with Kathryn O'Dell

2A

Workbook

CAMBRIDGE
UNIVERSITY PRESS

Contents

My interests

A *I'm interested in fashion.*

1 Complete the puzzle and the sentences with words for people's interests.

Across

3. I'm interested in ____*fashion*____ .
   I like new and different clothes.

4. Tonya is interested in _____ .
   She loves the old paintings at the museum.

8. Dennis is interested in _____ .
   His favorites are Spanish, Portuguese,
   and Chinese.

Down

1. Mario is interested in _____ .
   He likes basketball and soccer.

2. Jonathan is interested in _____ .
   He works with the president.

5. Mrs. Wilson doesn't like _____ .
   She hates computers!

6. Penny is interested in pop
   _____ . She loves popular music
   and art.

7. Are you interested in _____ ?
   Let's go to China for a month!

2 Match the questions and the answers.

1. Where is Daniel from? __e__
2. How old is Ricardo? _____
3. Is he married? _____
4. Is she interested in literature? _____
5. Are you interested in travel? _____
6. What's your name? _____
7. Where are they from? _____
8. What are you interested in? _____

a. Yes, she is.
b. My name's Sophia.
c. He's 24 years old.
d. They're from Colombia.
e. He's from Australia.
f. I'm interested in pop culture.
g. No, he isn't.
h. No, I'm not.

3 Look at Yolanda's information. Then answer the questions.

| Name: | Mrs. Yolanda Maria Gomez | Age: | 22 | Country: | Mexico |

What are you interested in? Do you want information about

Tell us about you.

sports?	● Yes, please.	○ No, thank you.	
	If yes, which sports?	soccer and tennis	
fashion?	○ Yes, please.	● No, thank you.	
politics?	● Yes, please.	○ No, thank you.	
travel?	● Yes, please.	○ No, thank you.	
	If yes, where?	China, Japan, and South Korea	
art?	○ Yes, please.	● No, thank you.	
pop culture?	○ Yes, please.	● No, thank you.	
literature?	● Yes, please.	○ No, thank you.	
languages?	● Yes, please.	○ No, thank you.	
	If yes, which languages?	Chinese, Japanese, and Korean	

1. What's Yolanda's last name?   _It's Gomez._____
2. Is she married?   _____
3. Is Maria her full name?   _____
4. How old is she?   _____
5. Where is she from?   _____
6. What sports is she interested in?   _____
7. Is she interested in Japanese?   _____
8. What countries is she interested in?   _____

4 Write about Yolanda's interests with the information from Exercise 3 on page 2. Use the simple present of *be*.

1. _Yolanda is interested in sports._
2. _She's not interested in fashion._
3. _____
4. _____
5. _____
6. _____
7. _____
8. _____

5 Complete the conversation with questions.

Lynne: Hello?

Judy: Hello. This is Judy from *Speak Magazine*.

Can I ask you some questions?

Lynne: Sure.

Judy: Thank you. _What's your name_ ?
                                        1

Lynne: I'm Lynne Roberts.

Judy: Hello, Ms. Roberts. _____ ?
                                                     2

Lynne: I'm from Chicago.

Judy: _____ ?
                      3

Lynne: I'm 31.

Judy: _____ or single?
                      4

Lynne: I'm married.

Judy: _____ ?
                      5

Lynne: My husband is 30 years old.

Judy: _____ ?
                      6

Lynne: Yes, we are. I'm interested in Spanish, and my husband speaks French.

Judy: Great. _____ ?
                              7

Lynne: Yes, we're interested in travel.

Judy: OK. Are you and your husband interested in *Speak Magazine*?

Lynne: Hmm . . .

B Can you repeat that, please?

1 Write the lines of the conversation in the correct order.

R-O-D-R-I-G-U-E-Z.
Hello, Gina. What's your last name?
Could you say that again, please?
Sure. Rodriguez.
✓Hi. This is Gina.
My last name is Rodriguez.
Oh, OK, Ms. Rodriguez. How do you spell that?

Gina: *Hi. This is Gina.* _____

Clerk: _____

Gina: _____

Clerk: _____

Gina: _____

Clerk: _____

Gina: _____

2 Complete the conversations with *repeat* or *more slowly*.

1. **A:** It's on page 122.

   B: Can you say that _*more slowly*_ , please?

2. **A:** What's your phone number?

   B: It's 324-555-1908.

   A: Could you speak _____ , please?

3. **A:** Her name is Na Young Park.

   B: Could you _____ that, please?

4. **A:** What's your last name?

   B: Lowery.

   A: Could you say that _____ , please?

5. **A:** The train is at 10:40 a.m.

   B: Can you _____ that, please?

C Do you play sports?

1 Label each picture with the correct word from the box.

baseball	golf	karate	swim	yoga
bowl	✓gymnastics	ski	table tennis	

UPTOWN SPORTS CENTER

1. _gymnastics_
Monday and Wednesday
2:00 p.m.

2. _____
Monday and Friday
5:00 p.m.

3. _____
Tuesday
7:00 a.m. and 4:00 p.m.

4. _____
Tuesday and Thursday
6:00 p.m.

5. _____
Wednesday
1:00 p.m. and 4:30 p.m.

6. _____
Thursday
6:30 p.m.

7. _____
Friday
3:30 p.m.

8. _____
Saturday
9:00 a.m.

9. _____
Saturday
2:30 p.m.

2 Complete the sentences with the words from Exercise 1. Use *play* or *do* when necessary.

1. You can _do gymnastics_ on Monday and Wednesday at 2:00 p.m.

2. You can _____ on Wednesday at 1:00 p.m. and 4:30 p.m.

3. You can _____ on Saturday at 9:00 a.m.

4. You can _____ on Tuesday at 7:00 a.m. and 4:00 p.m.

5. You can _____ on Friday at 3:30 p.m.

3 Put the words in the correct order to make questions and answers.

1. play / does / she / What / sports / ?   A: *What sports does she play?*

   table / plays / tennis / She / .   B: *She plays table tennis.*

2. gymnastics / they / do / Where / do / ?   A: _____

   school / do / at / They / gymnastics / .   B: _____

3. like / Does / he / karate / ?   A: _____

   he / Yes / , / does / .   B: _____

4. play / golf / When / do / you / ?   A: _____

   the / golf / I / play / in / morning / .   B: _____

5. you / Do / sell / skis / ?   A: _____

   don't / No / , / we / .   B: _____

6. they / afternoon / the / Do / swim / in / ?   A: _____

   don't / No / , / they / .   B: _____

4 Circle the correct words to complete the conversation.

Joe: Hey, Mari. Do you (like) / likes karate?
                                        1

Mari: No, I **doesn't** / **don't**. I **like** / **likes** yoga.
                      2   3

Joe: **Do** / **When do** you do yoga?
                      4

Mari: I usually **do** / **does** yoga after work.
                           5

   Do / **What do** you like yoga?
          6

Joe: No, I **do** / **don't**. But my brother **like** / **likes** it.
                7   8

Mari: **Do** / **Where do** you like golf?
                 9

Joe: Yes! I **play** / **plays** golf a lot. Do you
                       10

   do like / **like** golf?
          11

Mari: Yes, I **do** / **does**.
                      12

Joe: Great! Let's play golf on Saturday.

Mari: OK.

5 Complete the text with the simple present forms of the verbs in parentheses.

MINIATURE GOLF SCORECARD							

HOLE	Linda	Debbie	HOLE	Linda	Debbie
1	3	4	10	3	4
2	5	5	11	1	3
3	2	3	12	2	3
4	7	4	13	3	4
5	4	6	14	5	4
6	4	2	15	3	2
7	5	4	16	4	5
8	3	3	17	1	4
9	6	6	18	4	3
			Total	65*	69

Linda ____*likes*____ (like) the game miniature golf. A miniature golf course
1
_____ (have) 18 holes, but the course is very small. At the end of
2
the game, the person with the lowest score _____ (win).
3
Linda _____ (play) miniature golf with her friend Debbie. They
4
_____ (play) in the park on Saturdays, and Linda usually
5
_____ (win) the game. But that's OK with Debbie.
6
She _____ (like) the game, too, and they always
7
_____ (have) a lot of fun.
8

6 Read the text in Exercise 5. Use the answers below to complete the questions.

1. *What game does* _____ Linda like?   miniature golf
2. *Does a miniature golf course have* _____ 18 holes?   Yes, it does.
3. _____ with?   with her friend Debbie
4. _____ miniature golf?   in the park
5. _____ miniature golf?   on Saturdays
6. _____ the game, too?   Yes, she does.

7 Answer the questions about a sport you like.

1. What is the sport?   _____
2. When do you play it?   _____
3. Where do you play it?   _____

D Free time

1 Read the text. Check (✓) the events that are in a decathlon.

1. ☑ the 100-meter run   4. ☐ the 500-meter run

2. ☐ the high jump   5. ☐ the low jump

3. ☐ the 1500-meter hurdles   6. ☐ the long jump

The decathlon is a sports competition with ten different events. Athletes compete in all ten events for two days. After the ten events, the person with the best score wins.

There are four races, or track events, in the decathlon: the 100-meter run, the 400-meter run, the 1500-meter run, and the 110-meter hurdles. In the 110-meter hurdles, athletes run and jump. Athletes also compete in six field events. In the long jump, people run and jump. In the high jump, they run and jump over a high bar. In the pole vault, athletes run and jump over a high bar with a long pole. In the shot put, the javelin throw, and the discus throw, athletes throw different things. The shot is a large heavy ball. The javelin is a long thin pole. The discus is like a large round disk or plate.

The women's decathlon started in 2001. Before 2001, only men competed in the decathlon. Women now compete in the same ten events, but there are some differences. For example, the hurdles are lower and women jump over hurdles on a 100-meter course, not on a 110-meter course, like the men's decathlon. The shot, the javelin, and the discus in the women's decathlon are not as heavy as in the men's events.

2 Read the text again. Rewrite the sentences. Correct the underlined words.

1. The decathlon has <u>twelve</u> events.   *The decathlon has ten events.*

2. Athletes throw things in <u>five</u> events.   _____

3. The shot is a large heavy <u>disk</u>.   _____

4. <u>Women</u> jump over hurdles on a 110-meter course.   _____

5. The <u>men's</u> decathlon started in 2001.   _____

Descriptions

A He's talkative and friendly.

1 Put the letters in the correct order to make personality adjectives.

1. i y f l d r n e   *friendly*
2. v i t t k a a e l   _____
3. n i d f n e c t o   _____
4. n s u e o g r e   _____
5. y s h   _____

6. v c e i r t a e   _____
7. n u y f n   _____
8. g d n k w h r r a o i   _____
9. r s s u i e o   _____

2 Complete the sentences with some of the adjectives from Exercise 1. Use the simple present of *be*.

1. Ethan *is shy* but *confident* .

2. Rita _____ and _____ .

3. Tom and Ed _____ and _____ .

4. Paul and Yoko _____ _____ .

5. Ms. Perez _____ _____ .

6. Emma _____ _____ .

3 Rewrite the sentences with the words in parentheses.

1. Laura is shy but confident. (person)

   Laura is a shy but confident person.

2. Sue and Kelly are hardworking. (students)

   _____

3. Dana is talkative and funny. (girl)

   _____

4. He's serious but friendly. (guy)

   _____

5. She's generous. (mother)

   _____

6. They're creative and confident. (musicians)

   _____

7. I'm friendly. (person)

   _____

8. Mr. Nelson is talkative but serious. (teacher)

   _____

4 Complete the conversation with *What . . . like?* questions.

Doug: Hi, Isabel. How's your art class?

Isabel: I love it! My teacher is Mrs. Linden.

Doug: *What's she like* _____ ?
               ᵢ

Isabel: She's great. She's creative but serious. There are 12 students in the class.

Doug: _____ ?
               ₂

Isabel: They're shy, and they're not very friendly. But my friend John is in the class.

Doug: _____ ?
               ₃

Isabel: John is a talkative guy.

Doug: And _____ ?
                   ₄

Isabel: Me? I'm a serious and hardworking student!

5 Read Part 1 of Jenny's job evaluation. Then complete the evaluation in Part 2 with the simple present and the correct adjectives.

ACE ACCOUNTANTS
EMPLOYEE EVALUATION FORM

Employee's Name: _Jenny Lewis_   Job: _Accountant_   Date: _May 24_

Part 1: Which words describe the employee? Check the words.

☑ serious   ☑ confident   ☑ hardworking   ☑ creative

☐ talkative   ☐ funny   ☑ shy   ☑ friendly

Part 2: Write an evaluation of the employee.

Jenny _is a serious_ accountant and very _____ . She
          1   2
_____ . She works late every day. Jenny _____ person
          3   4
and has many good ideas. She is not very talkative or funny. Jenny _____
                                                                        5
but _____ . People like her.
          6

6 Write conversations for the pictures with your own ideas. Use *What . . . like?* questions and *be* + adjective (+ noun).

Examples: A: _What are they like?_   A: _What's he like?_
           B: _They're friendly but shy._   B: _He's a confident and creative actor._

The Jonas Brothers, singers and musicians

Johnny Depp, actor

1. A: _____ ?   2. A: _____ ?

   B: _____ .   B: _____ .

7 Write conversations for another actor or actress, singer or musician.

1. Actor or actress: _____   2. Singer or musician: _____

   A: _____ ?   A: _____ ?

   B: _____ .   B: _____ .

B I don't think so.

1 Circle the correct sentence to complete the conversation.

1. **A:** Is Mia hardworking?

   B: (I think so.) / I don't think so. She always works late.

2. **A:** Does your teacher give a lot of homework?

   B: I believe so. / I'm not really sure. It's the first day of class.

3. **A:** Is Jay-Jay talkative?

   B: I guess so. / I don't believe so. He's shy.

4. **A:** Are Mr. and Mrs. Trandall generous?

   B: I believe so. / I don't believe so. They sometimes help me.

2 Look at the pictures. Complete the conversations with expressions from Exercise 1. More than one answer is possible.

1. **A:** Is Larry funny?

   B: *I don't think so. / I don't believe so.*

2. **A:** Does Paula take a dance class?

   B: _____

3. **A:** Are Tina and Jordan friendly?

   B: _____

4. **A:** Does Eric like baseball?

   B: _____

C *What do they look like?*

1 Match the descriptions with the people in Joe's family. Then write about them.

A	B	C	D	E
young	middle-aged	bald	middle-aged	short and
tall and thin	long blond hair	a gray mustache	curly hair	overweight
wavy shoulder-	little round	elderly and	a short black	young
length hair	glasses	medium height	beard	straight black hair

1. This is my mother.

   She's middle-aged.

   She has long blond hair.

   She has little round glasses.

2. This is my grandfather.

   _____

   _____

3. These are my brothers.

   _____

   _____

   _____

4. This is my sister.

   _____

   _____

5. This is my father.

   _____

   _____

2 **Read the clues and label the pictures with the correct names.**

- Ken's hair isn't straight, long, or brown.
- Megan doesn't have short or black hair.
- Diane's hair isn't brown.
- Mario's hair isn't long or blond.

long black hair   short brown hair   wavy blond hair   straight blond hair

1. _____   2. _____   3. _____*Ken*_____   4. _____

3 **Answer the questions. Use the information from Exercise 2.**

1. What does Ken look like?   *He has wavy blond hair.* _____

2. What does Mario look like?   _____

3. What does Megan look like?   _____

4. What does Diane look like?   _____

4 **Look at the answers. Write the questions with *What . . . like?* or *What . . . look like?***

1. *What does he look like?* _____   He has a brown mustache.

2. *What's he like?* _____   He's confident and serious.

3. _____   She has long straight hair.

4. _____   They're tall and overweight.

5. _____   They're friendly and talkative people.

6. _____   I'm short and thin.

7. _____   He's pretty funny.

8. _____   I'm creative and hardworking.

9. _____   We have curly red hair.

5 Complete the chart with the words from the box.

black	curly	green	long		new	round	straight	wavy
blond	elderly	✓little	middle-aged		red	short	tall	young

Size	Age	Shape	Color
little			

6 Put the words in the correct order to make sentences.

1. hair / straight / John / has / brown / .   _John has straight brown hair._

2. short / He's / a / elderly / man / .   _____

3. round / Wendy / glasses / has / little / .   _____

4. have / eyes / green / They / small / .   _____

5. beard / long / He / a / has / gray / .   _____

6. We / hats / blue / new / have / .   _____

7 Look at the pictures. Write sentences. Use some of the words from Exercise 5.
More than one answer is possible.

1. _He has long curly_
   hair.
   He's young.

2. _____
   _____
   _____

3. _____
   _____
   _____

4. _____
   _____
   _____

1 Read the text. Write the name of the artist and the cartoon under the correct picture.

1. _____

2. _____

3. _____

Famous Cartoonists

Jim Davis

Jim Davis is famous for his comic strip, *Garfield*. It's about a cat named Garfield. This cat is lazy and eats a lot of lasagna. Garfield also sleeps a lot. Jim's comic is about a cat, but he doesn't have a pet cat now. Jim played with lots of cats when he was a boy. This helps him draw and write about Garfield. Jim lives and works in Muncie, Indiana.

Matt Groening

Matt Groening is famous for the cartoon *The Simpsons*. The characters in *The Simpsons* have the same names as the people in Matt's family, but they don't look like his family. The father in the cartoon, Homer, is bald. The mother, Marge, has big blue hair. Homer and Marge have three children. The sister, Lisa, is extremely serious, and Maggie is a baby. Bart is talkative and funny. Matt says Bart is like him. Matt is from Portland, Oregon, but he lives in Los Angeles now.

Cathy Guisewite

Cathy Guisewite also lives in Los Angeles, but she's from Dayton, Ohio. Her comic strip is *Cathy*. *Cathy* is about a woman's life. She and her mother do not always see things the same way. In the cartoon, Cathy likes to eat, and her mother thinks she's overweight. Cathy also has problems at work. The cartoon was about Cathy Guisewite, but now the real Cathy is married, and she has two children.

2 Read the text again. Then circle the correct answer.

1. Jim's cartoon is (*Garfield*) / *The Simpsons*.

2. The cartoon of Marge **looks like** / **doesn't look like** Matt's mother.

3. In *The Simpsons*, Lisa is very **serious** / **talkative**.

4. **Jim and Cathy** / **Matt and Cathy** live in Los Angeles now.

5. The real Cathy is **married** / **single**.

Rain or shine

A *It's extremely cold.*

1 Label each picture with the correct word from the box.

cloudy
✓cold
cool
hot
rainy
snowy
sunny
warm
windy

1. _____cold_____

2. _____

3. _____

4. _____

5. _____

6. _____

7. _____

8. _____

9. _____

2 Look at the map. Write sentences about the weather. Use the simple present of *be* and words from Exercise 1.

1. **Chicago**
2. **Detroit**
3. **Washington, D.C.**
4. **Atlanta**
5. **Miami**

1. _It's windy and cool in Chicago._____

2. _____

3. _____

4. _____

5. _____

3 Circle the correct answer for each picture.

1. What season is this?

   a. It's warm.

   b. It's the rainy season.

   c. It's the dry season.

2. What season do you like?

   a. I like summer.

   b. I like winter.

   c. I like fall.

3. What season is it now?

   a. It's the dry season.

   b. It's the rainy season.

   c. It's snowy.

4. What season is it in Toronto?

   a. It's winter.

   b. It's spring.

   c. It's summer.

5. What's your favorite season?

   a. It's fall.

   b. It's winter.

   c. It's the rainy season.

6. What season does he like?

   a. He likes sun.

   b. He likes winter.

   c. He likes spring.

4 Cross out the word that doesn't belong in each list.

1. extremely   really   ~~fairly~~   very

2. somewhat   a lot   pretty   fairly

3. summer   spring   sunny   fall

4. cold   warm   snowy   cool

5. summer   windy   snowy   rainy

6. cloudy   winter   sunny   snowy

5 Put the words in the correct order to make sentences.

1. very / winter / It's / cold / the / in / .   *It's very cold in the winter.*
2. spring / lot / in / It / rains / a / the / .   _____
3. New York City / windy / It's / pretty / in / .   _____
4. in / cool / It's / fairly / Quito / .   _____
5. season / in / It / dry / much / doesn't / rain / very / the / .   _____
6. summer / in / at / snow / It / doesn't / all / the / .   _____
7. a / It / Canada / bit / snows / quite / in / .   _____
8. extremely / It's / Bangkok / in / hot / .   _____

6 Circle the correct words to complete the sentences.

1. It's **(pretty)** / **a little** sunny today.
2. It rains **pretty** / **a lot** in London.
3. It's **extremely** / **a lot** hot in Istanbul.
4. It's **somewhat** / **very much** cool in March.
5. It doesn't snow **somewhat** / **very much** in Sydney.
6. It's **very** / **a lot** cloudy in Seattle.
7. It doesn't snow **extremely** / **at all** in Lima.
8. It's **at all** / **fairly** windy in Iceland.
9. It rains **a little** / **very** in December.
10. It's **really** / **quite a bit** hot in Mexico City.

7 Write about the weather in your town. Use the words in parentheses.

Example: (snow) *It snows a lot in the winter.* or *It doesn't snow at all.*

1. (snow)   _____
2. (rain)   _____
3. (windy)   _____
4. (hot)   _____
5. (sunny)   _____
6. (cloudy)   _____

B *In my opinion, . . .*

1 Complete the conversations with the words from the box.

I'd	opinion	think	thoughts	what	what's

A.   **Rosa:** Hey, Marcos. Let's have a party for Mom.

  Marcos: OK. When?

  Rosa: Hmm . . . I don't know. _____*What*_____ do you think?
                 1

  Marcos: I _____ Saturday is a good day.
            2

  Rosa: OK. That sounds good.

B.   **Jake:** Hi, Todd. When are you coming to see me?

  Todd: Well, I'm not sure. What are your _____ ?
               1

  Jake: In my _____ , winter is a good time. It usually
           2
       snows a lot. We can ski!

  Todd: OK. That would be great.

C.   **Hiro:** So, Julie. When is a good time for you to visit?

  Julie: _____ say in the winter. It's cold and snowy here.
          1

  Hiro: OK. Where should we meet?

  Julie: Hmm . . . _____ your opinion?
            2

  Hiro: How about Kyoto? Then you can meet my parents. It's somewhat cool in
       the winter, but it doesn't usually snow.

  Julie: That's a great idea!

2 Match the pictures to the conversations in Exercise 1. Label the pictures with the correct
conversation letter.

1. ☐

2. ☐

3. ☐

I'd like to play chess.

1 Complete the sentences with a word from each box. Use the simple present form of the verbs.

bake	✓do	make	play
do	make	play	take

a board game	✓a jigsaw puzzle	a video	cookies
a crossword	a nap	chess	popcorn

I usually _do a jigsaw puzzle_ _____ with
¹
my children.

Sometimes, we _____
²
with friends.

Sometimes, my wife and I _____
³
_____ on Friday evenings.

But we always _____
⁴
on Sunday mornings.

On Sunday afternoon, the kids _____
⁵
_____ .

And my mom _____
⁶
for us.

My wife _____ .
⁷

And I sometimes _____
⁸
like this one.

2 Look at the chart. Then answer the questions.

Healthy Pines Recreation Center

		Activities for Wednesday Afternoon			
NAME	**PLAY CHESS**	**PLAY A BOARD GAME**	**DO A JIGSAW PUZZLE**	**BAKE COOKIES**	**DO YOGA**
Ethan			✓		
Carolyn	✓				
Paul	✓				
Marina				✓	
Emma		✓			
Doug		✓			
Jenny					✓
Mark					✓

1. What would Ethan like to do? <u>*He'd like to do a jigsaw puzzle.*</u>

2. Would Carolyn and Paul like to play chess? <u>*Yes, they'd like to play chess.*</u>

3. What would Marina like to do? _____

4. Would Emma like to bake cookies? _____

5. Would Doug like to play a board game? _____

6. What would Jenny and Mark like to do? _____

3 Look at the answers. Write the questions about the underlined parts.

1. <u>*What would she like to play?*</u>   She'd like to play <u>a board game</u>.

2. _____   He'd like <u>to take a nap</u>.

3. _____   I'd like to play <u>baseball</u>.

4. _____   <u>No, they wouldn't</u>. They don't like gymnastics.

5. _____   I'd like to do yoga <u>in the park</u>.

6. _____   <u>Yes, she would</u>. She loves chess.

7. _____   <u>No, I wouldn't</u>. I never take naps.

8. _____   They'd like to make a video <u>at the school</u>.

4 Write sentences about what the people would like and wouldn't like to do.

1. Kara _would like to play table tennis._

   She wouldn't like to play soccer.

2. Dan _____

   _____

3. Sheila and Greg _____

   _____

4. Mr. and Mrs. Jones _____

   _____

5. Larry _____

   _____

6. Claudia _____

   _____

5 Answer the questions with your own information.

1. Would you like to play chess tonight?   _____

2. Would you like to take a nap on Saturday?   _____

3. Would you like to play soccer tomorrow?   _____

4. Would you like to do your homework in a park? _____

5. Where would you like to go for vacation?   _____

6. When would you like to go to bed?   _____

D *Where would you like to go?*

1 Read the email. Write the names of the places and the weather under the correct pictures.

1. _____Otavalo_____ 2. _____ 3. _____ 4. _____

   _____cool_____   _____   _____   _____

   _____pretty cold_____ _____   _____   _____

Hi, Rachel!

I'm having a great time in Ecuador with my family. We're in Quito right now. It's the capital of Ecuador. The city is big, and there's a lot to do. It's warm in the day and cool at night now. It sometimes rains a lot in Quito, but it's not the rainy season now. We're walking around the city a lot.

The weather is really different in other parts of Ecuador. In the town of Otavalo, the weather is cool all day and pretty cold at night. There's a famous market in Otavalo with many handmade clothes. We went to Otavalo on Monday. We got beautiful sweaters at the market to wear at night!

There are a lot of beaches in Ecuador. The beaches are usually sunny and very hot. We went to a beach in Muisne on Wednesday and had a great time! It was sunny and hot!

Cotopaxi National Park is close to Quito. The park is very big, and it has a large volcano in it. The volcano is also called Cotopaxi. It snows quite a bit on Cotopaxi, and it's extremely cold and snowy at the top. You can walk to the top. The kids can't do it, but Helena and I would like to walk up there this weekend.

How are you? Say hi to Mike and the kids.

Your friend,
Martin

---

2 Read the email again. Then write T (true), F (false), or NI (no information).

1. Quito is the capital of Ecuador. ___T___

2. There isn't a market in Quito. _____

3. Martin and his family liked the beach in Muisne. _____

4. Martin's children are very young. _____

5. Martin and Helena are in Cotopaxi National Park now. _____

6. Rachel would like to go to Ecuador. _____

Life at home

A *There's a lot of light.*

1 Cross out the word that doesn't usually belong in each list.

1. **bedroom:** dresser closet ~~dishwasher~~
2. **bathroom:** sink sofa shower
3. **living room:** armchair coffee table toilet
4. **kitchen:** bathtub refrigerator cupboards
5. **bedroom:** curtains stove bed

2 Complete the sentences with some of the words from Exercise 1.

STUFF FOR **SALE**

I'm selling my _____**bed**_____
                    1
and _____ . They're
          2
two years old. $150.

For sale: an old
_____ . $50.
        3
Email r27@cup.org.

We're selling our
_____ and
        4
_____ . Click
        5
here to respond.

House for sale. Two bedrooms,
a big _____ with a
              6
dishwasher.

I can make _____
                      7
for your bedroom or
living room! Call Susie
at 222-5678.

I can fix your _____
                          8
and _____ !
          9
Email Jason at Jfix@cup.com.

3 What's in your home? Complete the chart with the words from the box.

Example: **Kitchen** *three cupboards, a sink, a refrigerator*

armchair	closet	curtains	refrigerator	sink
bathtub	coffee table	dishwasher	shelves	sofa
bed	cupboards	dresser	shower	stove

Living Room	Kitchen	Bedroom	Bathroom

4 Write about your home. Use *some, a few, many,* and *any* and the words in parentheses.

Example: <u>There are a few cupboards in my kitchen.</u> or
<u>There aren't many cupboards in my kitchen.</u>

1. (cupboards / kitchen) _____

2. (shelves / bedroom) _____

3. (armchairs / living room) _____

4. (closets / house) _____

5. (bedrooms / house) _____

5 Circle the correct word or phrase to complete each sentence about Sandra's house.

1. There's (a lot of)/ **many** noise on the street.

2. There's **some** / **a few** light in the living room.

3. There isn't **many** / **any** space in the closets.

4. There's **a little** / **a few** light in the bedroom.

5. There aren't **many** / **a little** cupboards in the kitchen.

6. There are **much** / **a few** shelves in the bathroom.

6 Complete the questions with *much* or *many.*

1. How _____ *much* _____ light is there in the kitchen?

2. How _____ closets are there in the bedrooms?

3. Are there _____ shelves in the closets?

4. How _____ street noise is there?

5. Is there _____ space in the kitchen?

7 Complete the conversation with the questions from Exercise 6.

Mr. Clark: So, this is the house for sale.

Andrew: Oh, it's nice. _How much street noise is there?_
1

Mr. Clark: Oh, it's fairly quiet.

Lydia: Now about the house!

_____
2

Mr. Clark: There's quite a bit of light.

Andrew: That's good. We love cooking.

_____
3

Mr. Clark: No, not really. It's pretty small, but there are a lot of cupboards.

Lydia: And the bedrooms? _____
4

Mr. Clark: There are two closets in the big bedroom, and there's one closet in

the small bedroom.

Andrew: Oh, that's good. _____
5

Mr. Clark: I'm not sure about the shelves. Let's look at the house!

Lydia: That's a good idea!

8 Read the answers. Then write the questions.

1. _How much noise is there in the living room?_   There isn't any noise in the living room.

2. _____   There is some light in the bathroom.

3. _____   There are a lot of cupboards in the kitchen.

4. _____   There isn't much space in the dresser.

5. _____   There are a few shelves in the bedroom.

6. _____   Yes, there are four armchairs in the

living room.

B Can you turn down the music?

1 Check (✓) all the words that complete the request.

_____ you open this cupboard, please?

☑ Could ☐ How ☐ When ☐ Where

☐ Would ☐ Do ☐ Can

2 Check (✓) all the responses to the request in Exercise 1.

☑ No problem. ☐ Oh, really? ☐ A little.

☐ In my opinion. ☐ Sure. ☐ I'd be happy to.

3 Complete the request and the response in each conversation. Use different words and expressions from Exercises 1 and 2.

A. Karen: Hey, Jeff. It's Karen from upstairs.

Would you turn down

1
your TV, please? It's too noisy, and I'm studying.

Jeff: _____ .

2
Sorry about the noise.

Karen: Thanks.

B. Tessa: It's hot in here.

Megan: I know. _____

1
the window, please?

Tessa: _____ .

2

Megan: Thanks. That's better.

C. Don: Hey, Liv.

_____

1
the phone?

Liv: _____ .

2

Don: Thanks. I can't talk right now.

C I always hang up my clothes!

1 Complete the household chores with *away, off, out,* or *up.*

1. wipe _____*off*_____ the counter
2. take _____ the garbage
3. hang _____ the clothes
4. clean _____ the yard
5. drop _____ the dry cleaning
6. pick _____ the magazines
7. put _____ the dishes
8. clean _____ the closets

2 What household chores can you do with these items? Label the pictures with some of the phrases from Exercise 1.

1. _clean up the yard_____   2. _____   3. _____

4. _____   5. _____   6. _____

3 Rewrite the sentences.

1. Please pick up those magazines.   _Please pick those magazines up._

2. Can you take out the garbage?   _____

3. Dennis cleans his yard up every week.   _____

4. I usually put away the dishes at night.   _____

5. Would you drop this letter off at the post office?   _____

6. My son and daughter never hang their clothes up.   _____

4 Complete the answers with the phrasal verb and *it* or *them*.

1. Where do you drop off your dry cleaning?   I _drop it off_____ at Super Clean.

2. Where do you hang your coat up?   I _____ in the closet.

3. Who can clean up the living room?   David can _____ .

4. Who can clean out the closets?   Marta and Vern can _____ .

5. Do your children put away their toys?   No, they don't _____ .

6. Does your husband take the garbage out?   No, I _____ .

7. How often do you wipe off the counters?   I _____ three times a day.

8. How often does Miho clean the garage out?   She _____ once a year.

5 Rewrite the questions in Exercise 4 with *it* or *them*.

1. _Where do you drop it off?_____

2. _____

3. _____

4. _____

5. _____

6. _____

7. _____

8. _____

6 Look at the chart. Who does each chore? Write two sentences about each chore. Use *it* or *them* in the second sentence.

	Sunday	Monday	Tuesday	Wednesday	Thursday	Friday	Saturday
1. put the dishes away				Kelly and Tim			Dad
2. take out the garbage			Dad			Kelly	
3. drop off the dry cleaning		Mom				Tim	
4. pick up the dry cleaning	Kelly			Dad			
5. hang the clothes up			Kelly		Tim		
6. clean up the yard		Mom and Kelly					Dad and Tim
7. clean up the bathrooms			Mom and Tim			Kelly	
8. clean out the cars	Kelly and Tim			Mom and Dad			

1. _Kelly and Tim put the dishes away on Wednesday._   _Dad puts them away on Saturday._

2. _____   _____

3. _____   _____

4. _____   _____

5. _____   _____

6. _____   _____

7. _____   _____

8. _____   _____

7 Answer the questions with your own information. Use *it* or *them*.

1. Who takes out the garbage in your home? _____

2. How often do you wipe off the counters in your kitchen? _____

3. When do you put away the dishes? _____

4. How often do you drop off the dry cleaning? _____

5. Where do you hang up your clothes? _____

6. How often do you clean up the kitchen? _____

D *What a home!*

1 Read the article. Then complete each sentence with one word.

1. Jake: "When I travel, my bed is on a _____ ."

2. Maria: "When I travel, I sleep in a _____ bed."

3. Tom and Riana: "The virtual _____ is very clean."

Other Homes

Do you have another place you call "home"? Four people describe their "other homes."

JAKE LONDON'S TOUR BUS

I'm a musician. I play the guitar and sing. I travel quite a bit with my band, so my other home is a big bus. There's a kitchen and a bathroom on the bus. There's a small living room with a TV. There are six beds on the bus, one for each person in the band!

MARIA MILLER'S HOTEL ROOM

I'm a flight attendant. Because of my job, I stay in hotels a lot. The hotel rooms usually have a big bed, a small kitchen, and a desk. So, hotel rooms are my "other homes." I always bring a few personal items when I travel for work. I take a nice dress, a few T-shirts, and my favorite jeans. I take a small pillow, and I always take a good book. I'm usually in one place only for a day, so I can put my things away in five minutes!

TOM AND RIANA PETERSON'S VIRTUAL HOUSE

Our "other home" isn't real! We love computer games. We play a game on our computer in a virtual world. We have avatars in this virtual world, and they have a home! Our real home is a small apartment, but the virtual house is big. In the virtual home, our avatars do the household chores. They clean up the rooms, put away the dishes, and take the garbage out. The virtual house is very clean, but our real house is a mess!

2 Read the text again. Answer the questions.

1. What does Jake do? *He's a musician.* _____

2. Is there a TV on Jake's bus? _____

3. What does Maria do? _____

4. How much time is Maria usually in one place? _____

5. Who does the household chores in Tom and Riana's virtual home? _____

Health

A Breathe deeply.

1 Label the parts of the body with the correct words from the box.

ankle	eye	hand	leg	nose	teeth
arm	finger	✓head	mouth	shoulder	toe
ear	foot	knee	neck	stomach	wrist

1. _____ *head*
2. _____
3. _____
4. _____
5. _____
6. _____
7. _____
8. _____
9. _____
10. _____
11. _____
12. _____
13. _____
14. _____
15. _____
16. _____
17. _____
18. _____

2 Match the objects to the corresponding parts of the body. Label each picture with the correct word from the box.

✓back	eyes	feet	finger	neck	wrist

1. _____back_____   2. _____   3. _____

4. _____   5. _____   6. _____

3 Complete the instructions with the correct form of the verb in parentheses.

TIPS for Using Crutches

1. _____Walk_____ (walk) slowly.

2. _____ (not look) down.

3. _____ (wear) good shoes.

4. _____ (practice) with a friend.

5. _____ (not walk) on snowy streets.

6. _____ (not open) doors.

_____ (ask) a friend for help.

7. _____ (have) a friend move chairs and tables in your home.

8. _____ (be) careful!

4 Complete the chart with the correct adverbs.

Adjective	Adverb
1. careful	*carefully*
2. deep	
3. heavy	
4. noisy	
5. quick	
6. quiet	
7. slow	

5 Circle the correct adverb to complete each sentence.

1. Raise your arms _____ .
   a. noisily   b. deeply   (c.) quickly

2. Please talk _____ in the library.
   a. slowly   b. quietly   c. noisily

3. Walk _____ , please. I can't walk quickly.
   a. heavily   b. slowly   c. quietly

4. Don't breathe _____ . Breathe deeply and relax.
   a. heavily   b. quietly   c. carefully

5. Lower your head _____ .
   a. heavily   b. noisily   c. carefully

6. Breathe _____ in yoga. Relax and breathe slowly.
   a. deeply   b. noisily   c. quickly

6 Write sentences with the words in parentheses. Use the simple present or the imperative form of the verbs and the adverb form of the adjectives.

1. *Jim stretches slowly.* _____ (Jim / stretch / slow)
2. _____ (breathe / deep / for ten minutes)
3. _____ (not breathe / heavy)
4. _____ (Millie / talk / quiet / on the phone)
5. _____ (not walk / quick / after lunch)
6. _____ (we / listen / careful / to our teacher)

7 Answer the questions with your own information.

Example: _I talk quickly._ or _I talk slowly._

1. Do you talk slowly or quickly? _____

2. Do you drive quickly or carefully? _____

3. Do you walk quietly or noisily? _____

B I'm not feeling well.

1 Complete the puzzle with words for health problems. What's the mystery word?

 1.
 2.
 3.
 4.

 5.
 6.
 7.

2 Complete each conversation with two different expressions from the box.

Get well soon.	I feel awful.	✓I'm not feeling well.
I don't feel so good.	I hope you feel better.	Take it easy.

A. Ed: Hi, Pat. How are you?

   Pat: *I'm not feeling well.*
   _____
   1

   Ed: What's wrong?

   Pat: I have a bad cough.

   Ed: That's too bad. _____
   2

B. Meg: Hey, Tim. How are you?

   Tim: _____
   1

   Meg: What's wrong?

   Tim: I have the flu.

   Meg: Oh, no! _____
   2

C How healthy are you?

1 Put the letters in the correct order to make phrases about healthy habits.

1. t a e   a   a b l n a d e c   t i d e

   eat a balanced diet

2. t t p e o c r   u y o r   s i n k

   _____

3. t e a   a   o g o d   f r a e s k b a t

   _____

4. t g e   g n h u e o   p e s e l

   _____

5. s r e e e c x i   i d y l a

   _____

6. s h a w   y r o u   d a s h n

   _____

7. o g   r f o   a   k l w a

   _____

8. f l i t   g w s i e t h

   _____

2 Look at the pictures. How often do you do these things? Write sentences about your habits using some of the phrases from Exercise 1 and *always, usually, hardly ever,* or *never.*

Example: _I usually eat a balanced diet._

1. _____

2. _____

3. _____

4. _____

5. _____

6. _____

3 Complete the questions with *How long, How many, How much, How often,* or *How well.*

1. *How many*_____ vegetables do you eat at dinner?   Hmm . . . Not many.

2. _____ do you walk in the mornings?   For about 30 minutes.

3. _____ do you play soccer?   Pretty well.

4. _____ meals do you cook a week?   Ten meals.

5. _____ coffee do you drink each day?   Two or three cups.

6. _____ do you do karate?   Once a week.

7. _____ do you do yoga?   For about an hour.

8. _____ sleep do you get?   Quite a bit.

4 Look at Greg's answers to an online health quiz. Write the questions.

ooo

ARE YOU HEALTHY?
Choose the answers that best describe your habits.

1. **Q:** *How often do you eat breakfast?*_____

   A: I eat breakfast *every day*.

2. **Q:** _____

   A: I follow my diet *pretty well*.

3. **Q:** _____

   A: I exercise *daily*.

4. **Q:** _____

   A: I drink *a lot* of water.

5. **Q:** _____

   A: I *don't get much* sleep.

6. **Q:** _____

   A: I wash my hands *three times* a day.

7. **Q:** _____

   A: My eating habits are *somewhat healthy*.

8. **Q:** _____

   A: I spend *four hours a day* at the gym.

5 Write questions with *How* and the words in parentheses to complete the conversation. Use the answers to help you.

Tae Ho: Hi, Fran. How is your mom feeling?

Fran: She's not well. She's always tired and doesn't eat well.

Tae Ho: *How much fruit does she eat?* (fruit / eat)
1

Fran: A lot. She eats apples or bananas every day.

Tae Ho: _____ (eat / vegetables)
2

Fran: She always eats vegetables at dinner.

Tae Ho: _____ (meals / eat / a day)
3

Fran: Two. Breakfast and dinner. Is that OK?

Tae Ho: Well, three is better. _____
4
(go to the gym)

Fran: About three times a week.

Tae Ho: _____ (spend at the gym)
5

Fran: Oh, about an hour. She lifts weights, and she does yoga.

Tae Ho: _____ (sleep / get)
6

Fran: About four hours a night.

Tae Ho: That's not much sleep. In my opinion, that's why she's always tired!

6 Rewrite the questions from Exercise 5 with *you*. Then answer the questions with your own information.

1. *How much fruit do you eat* _____ ?

   I _____ .

2. _____ ?

   _____ .

3. _____ ?

   _____ .

4. _____ ?

   _____ .

5. _____ ?

   _____ .

6. _____ ?

   _____ .

D *Don't stress out!*

Read the text. Write the instructions from the box in the correct places.

Move your arms to the right.	Sit carefully on the ball.
Raise your body.	Then lower your head and arms.

The New **HealthyYou** Exercise Ball

Repeat these exercises 20 times for each activity.

THE SIT UP

1. Put your back carefully on the ball. Place your feet on the floor.
2. Put your hands behind your head.
3. Raise your head and arms slowly. Hold your stomach in.
4. _____

THE WEIGHT LIFT

1. _____
   Place your feet on the floor.
2. Hold a weight in each hand.
3. Lift the weights over your head. Keep your back straight.
4. Lower the weights to your shoulders.

THE REACH

1. Stand up and hold the ball. Stretch your arms and raise the ball over your head.
2. Move your arms to the left. Keep your legs straight. Don't move your feet.
3. _____

THE SQUAT

1. Place the ball against the wall. Put your back against the wall.
2. Lower your body, bending your knees. Keep your back straight.
3. _____

What's on TV?

A I love watching game shows.

1 Look at the pictures. Circle the correct answer.

1. What type of shows do they like?
   a. Documentaries
   b. Cartoons
   c. Talk shows

2. What type of shows does Jim watch?
   a. Reality shows
   b. Sitcoms
   c. Cartoons

3. What's his favorite type of TV show?
   a. Game shows
   b. The news
   c. Soap operas

4. What do they watch at night?
   a. The news
   b. Talk shows
   c. Dramas

5. What type of shows does his family watch?
   a. Sitcoms
   b. Documentaries
   c. Game shows

6. What does Sarah watch after work?
   a. Sitcoms
   b. Dramas
   c. The news

7. What's on TV?
   a. A game show
   b. A cartoon
   c. A talk show

8. What's that?
   a. A cartoon
   b. A reality show
   c. A soap opera

9. What are they watching?
   a. The news
   b. A drama
   c. A talk show

2 Complete the chart. Write the verbs from the box in the correct column.

dislike	✓hate	like	prefer
enjoy	hope	love	want

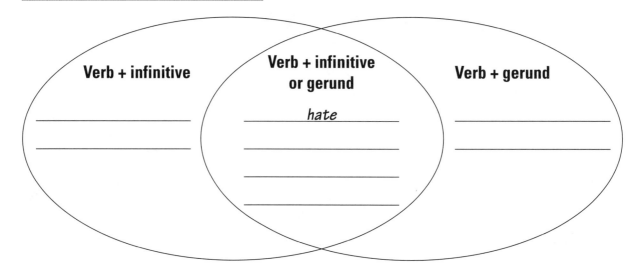

Verb + infinitive

_____

_____

Verb + infinitive or gerund

____hate____

_____

_____

_____

Verb + gerund

_____

_____

3 Put the words in the correct order to make sentences.

1. at night / shows / watch / I / like / reality / to / .

   I like to watch reality shows at night.

2. to / new / Melvin / buy / TV / next week / hopes / a / .

   _____

3. on the Internet / TV shows / dislikes / My / mother / watching / .

   _____

4. do / What / love / of TV shows / types / watching / you / ?

   _____

5. favorite / hate / We / our / missing / show / .

   _____

6. on the radio / listen / Sarah and Mike / prefer / to / to the news / .

   _____

4 In four of the sentences from Exercise 3, the verb can be followed by either a gerund or an infinitive. Rewrite those sentences in the other way.

1. _I like watching reality shows at night._

2. _____

3. _____

4. _____

5 Answer the questions with the words in parentheses. Use the correct form of the verbs. Sometimes two answers are possible.

1. What shows do you watch on TV?

   <u>*I love watching sitcoms. / I love to watch sitcoms.*</u>   (love / watch / sitcoms)

2. Does your sister like reality shows?

   Yes. _____ (enjoy / watch / them)

3. Do you listen to the radio?

   No, I don't. _____ (prefer / listen / to music on my computer)

4. Why is Jack at the store?

   _____ (want / buy / a new TV)

5. Why is Laura at the bookstore?

   _____ (hope / see / that famous writer)

6. What types of movies does Paul like?

   _____ (like / watch / dramas)

7. Why aren't Dan and Susan at the mall?

   _____ (hate / shop)

8. Do you and Mary watch a lot of TV?

   No. _____ (dislike / watch / TV)

6 Circle the correct words to complete the conversation.

Mara: Hey, Ken. What's wrong?

Ken: Well, I (hate) / dislike to watch TV.
                    1

Mara: Oh, OK. What do you **enjoy** / **want** to do?
                                        2

Ken: Hmm . . . Well, I **like** / **want** riding bikes.
                                3

Mara: But it's really cold outside!

Ken: You're right. I **hope** / **enjoy** playing board games.
                            4

Mara: Well, I **prefer** / **enjoy** to play chess.
                    5

Ken: OK. Let's play chess! Could you turn off the TV?

Mara: Well, actually . . . I **want** / **dislike** to watch it
                                6
   while we play.

Ken: Oh, no!

B I don't really agree.

1 Complete the conversation with *agree* or *disagree*.

Tim: I think cartoons are great!

Aisha: I _____agree_____ . They're funny!

1

Wendy: I don't really _____ , Aisha.

2
Cartoons aren't funny. They're boring.

Aisha: Wendy, don't you like soap operas?

Wendy: Yes, I do. Why?

Aisha: Well, I think soap operas are boring!

Wendy: I _____ . They're interesting!

3

Tim: I'm afraid I _____ , Wendy.

4
They are pretty boring!

Wendy: Well, what do you think of reality shows?

Tim: Oh, they're great . . . interesting and funny!

Aisha: I _____ with you, Tim!

5

Wendy: Hey, I think so, too. Let's watch a reality show.

2 Complete the conversations with your opinion. Use some of the expressions from Exercise 1.

A. **Tim:** I think cartoons are great.

Aisha: I think so, too. They're funny.

You: _____

1
Wendy: I think cartoons are boring.

You: _____

2

B. **Aisha:** Do you like soap operas?

Wendy: Yes! I think soap operas are interesting!

You: _____

1
Tim: I think soap operas are boring!

You: _____

2

C I'm recording a documentary.

1 Complete the sentences and the puzzle with television words.

Across

2. Jenny likes to watch _____ of old sitcoms on TV. She watches the same shows from the 1990s every night.

5. Do you _____ the sad parts of movies? I never watch them.

6. I'm going to work. Can you _____ my favorite show? Thanks!

7. I like watching TV shows online. I _____ through the boring parts!

Down

1. I don't pay for any TV channels, but there are some good shows on _____ *public* _____ TV.

2. Where's the _____ control? I want to turn the TV on.

3. Do you have _____ TV? You have great channels, but I didn't see a dish outside.

4. I hate watching TV. I like the shows, but I don't like the _____ .

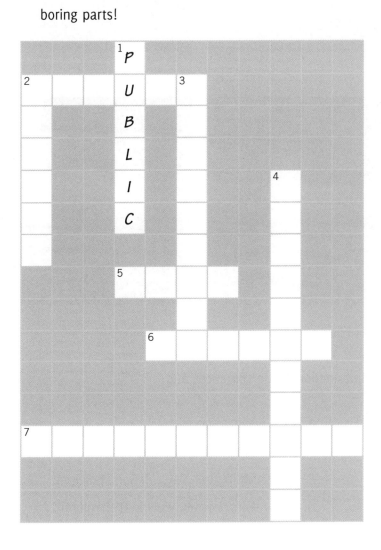

2 **What are they doing on Saturday? Read the sentences. Label the pictures with the correct names.**

- Tom is staying home on Saturday.
- Tonya is taking her school books to the library on Saturday.
- Isabella is going to a club on Saturday.
- Randy is playing a sport on Saturday.
- Emily is driving to her sister's house on Saturday.
- Mateo is meeting a friend at a Japanese restaurant on Saturday.

1. _____*Isabella*_____   2. _____   3. _____

4. _____   5. _____   6. _____

3 **Match the questions and answers. Use the information in the sentences and the pictures in Exercise 2.**

1. What's Tom doing on Saturday? __*e*__   a. He's playing soccer.

2. What's Randy doing on Saturday? _____   b. He's eating sushi with Naoki.

3. What's Isabella doing on Saturday? _____   c. She's visiting her sister in San Francisco.

4. What's Emily doing on Saturday? _____   d. She's doing her homework at the library.

5. What's Mateo doing on Saturday? _____   e. He's watching TV.

6. What's Tonya doing on Saturday? _____   f. She's going dancing.

4 Rewrite the sentences. Use the present continuous and the words in parentheses.

1. She goes to work.

   _She's going to work on Monday_____ . (on Monday)

2. He watches reruns of his favorite TV show.

   _____ . (tonight)

3. What do you do for fun?

   _____ ? (this weekend)

4. Does he teach English in South Korea?

   _____ ? (next year)

5. We don't record our favorite shows.

   _____ . (on Friday)

6. The Hawks play the Lions.

   _____ . (next week)

7. I don't cook Mexican food.

   _____ . (for the party)

8. Where does she travel for work?

   _____ ? (next month)

5 Look at some of Becky's plans for next week. Then read the answers and complete the questions.

Thursday	Friday	Saturday	Sunday
- buy a new TV	- have a party for Mark - make and post a video of the party	- watch the baseball game with Tim - record the game for Doug	- visit my parents - go out with Joan

1. _Is Becky buying a new TV_____ on Friday?   No, she isn't. She's buying it on Thursday.

2. _____ on Sunday?   No, they aren't. They're watching it on Saturday.

3. _____ on Saturday?   No, she isn't. She's having it on Friday.

4. _____ of the game?   No, she isn't. She's making a video of the party.

5. _____ for Mark?   No, she isn't. She's recording it for Doug.

6. _____ on Thursday?   No, they aren't. They are going out on Sunday.

7. _____ her grandparents?   No, she isn't. She's visiting her parents.

8. _____ on Saturday?   No, she isn't. She's visiting them on Sunday.

D Popular TV

1 Read the article. Write the headings for each section in the correct place.

> Watch on your cell phone   Watch on your computer   Watch on your TV

○ ○ ○ How are you watching your favorite TV shows?

1. _____

You like watching shows on your TV at home, but you don't want to pay a lot of money. In the past, most TV programs were free. Now you have to pay for many TV channels. Satellite dishes are expensive, too. Get a digital video player. It's a small box, and it's not very expensive. Connect it to your TV, and you can watch shows from the Internet on your TV for free!

2. _____

You can watch many TV shows online. For example, one website has TV shows from the United States and England. Another website has TV shows from around the world. Do you like reruns? On some websites you can watch old TV shows. Watch all the episodes of an entire year of your favorite show in one weekend!

Some TV networks have their own TV programs online. These programs have a series of episodes. The episodes of these TV programs are often online for only a few weeks. Then the networks remove the old episodes and add new ones. There are also some commercials, but they are usually short.

3. _____

You are never home and you don't like to take your computer everywhere with you. You can download TV shows from a website to your computer. Then download them from your computer to your phone. It is even possible to download or stream some TV shows directly into some types of cell phones. You can watch the shows on a bus, or on a train, or while you are exercising at the gym!

> TV is almost 100 years old! Here are some important dates in the history of television.
> • **1920s** first TV sets
> • **1930s** first TV commercial
> • **1940s** first sitcom, first color TV sets
> • **1950s** first reality show
> • **1960s** first satellite TV

2 Read the article again. Then answer the questions.

1. Are reality shows new?   _No, they aren't._____

2. Do shows online have commercials?   _____

3. Can you watch reruns online?   _____

4. How can you watch TV shows on a bus? _____

5. What can you connect to your TV to watch shows from the Internet?   _____

Credits